gift

Maria Szapszewicz

For The People I Love

And

Can't Forget

·

Poems and Memories
of the
Holocaust

Jacob's House
Press

Copyright © 2006 by Maria Szapszewicz

Editor: Robert J. Hutcheson, Ph.D.

Illustrator: Joanne Szapszewicz-Scott

Art Director/Designer: Jim Murphy

Library of Congress Control Number: 2006901017

ISBN 13: 978-0-9778604-0-1
ISBN 10: 0-9778604-0-X

First Edition

*With best wishes
and love
Mona Shopsowitz*

Dedication

To my dear husband Jacob
To my daughters Rose and Joanne
And to my most precious grandchildren
Marisa and Ariella and my son-in-law Gary

Table of Contents

Essays, Stories and an Interview on the Holocaust

FOREWORD

The Second World War of the twentieth century was the worst human-devised tragedy in history. Nearly 30,000,000 human beings died in the six-year period of that war. Most of them were soldiers fighting in uniform with the weapons of war—tanks, ships and aircraft. Others were civilian victims of the conflict, the inhabitants of cities firebombed or smashed by atom bombs. And millions were victims of Nazi racism, mainly Jews, murdered in the fields behind advancing German armies, or gassed in German murder marts.

I served as a line officer in the United States Navy throughout World War II. Towards the end of the war, I was assigned for special duty with the Office of Strategic Services, or OSS, and was placed in charge of the investigation of war crimes in the European Theater. While on this assignment in Europe, I came in contact with the small European staff which had been assembled by the United States Chief of Counsel, Supreme Court Justice Robert H. Jackson, in London. I was invited to join the prosecution team and moved with the others to Nuremberg, Germany, where the trial of the major German war criminals was to be held, in August 1945.

The principal repressive agency of the Nazi regime was the Reich Main Security Office. Both intelligence and special police agencies were combined in this office. Since I had acquired some knowledge of the Nazi intelligence system while serving in OSS, I was assigned the case against the Gestapo and SD, two repressive organizations within the RSHA, and against its Chief, Ernst Kaltenbrunner.

The major crime against humanity charged to the Nuremberg defendants was the extermination of the Jews of Europe, along with Gypsies and other minority groups. This crime was primarily the responsibility of the Gestapo and SD within the Government and of the SS within the Party. Thus, this part of the case fell into my hands.

No record has been found of any written order by Hitler directing the annihilation of the Jews of Europe. But, from his public utterances, it is clear that he intended their total destruction as part of his plan for the seizure of the Eastern territories and eventual Germanic rule of the European continent.

The Nazi extermination program was carried out in two principal ways—by Einsatzgruppen which murdered approximately 2,000,000 victims in the open fields, and through concentration camps in which approximately 4,000,000 persons were murdered. I was able to develop proof of these crimes through individuals directly responsible for both forms of murder—Otto Ohlendorf, the chief of the SD inside Germany, who headed Einsatzgruppen D, and Rudolf Hoess, the commander of Auschwitz concentration camp, in which Maria and her mother suffered but miraculously survived. After we finished with Hoess at Nuremberg, he was turned over to Polish authorities. He was tried and convicted by the supreme Polish tribunal in Warsaw and hanged on the grounds of Auschwitz. The gallows still stand there as a silent remembrance of the Auschwitz massacres and the man who directed the killing of innocents in that tomb of terror.

To learn through her poetic writings of the tragic life of Maria and her loved ones, who died or suffered under the Nazi Inquisition, is to comprehend the dreadful frailties of the human character in this period of history. Let us pray that the centuries to come will see the end of man's inhumanity to man.

> *Maria, Maria*
> *Child of the Twentieth Century.*
> *You suffered in Auschwitz,*
> *You almost died in Bergen-Belsen.*
> *What are these places?*
> *Are they not samples of Hell on Earth*
> *Helping us to visualize*
> *The Ultimate Hell there is to be*
> *For the Nazi Murderers of the twentieth century?*

Whitney R. Harris
Author, *Tyranny on Trial*

Author's Foreword

My name is Maria Szapszewicz (née Wajchendler). I was born in Lodz, Poland to very loving parents, Sara and Majlech Wajchendler, and had two brothers, Henry and Leon. Along with many other members of our extended family, my brothers and our father perished in the Holocaust.

I lived in two ghettoes during World War II, those of Lodz and Szydlowiec. I was forced to work in an ammunition factory in Starachowice; then, I was sent to Auschwitz and, later, to the Bergen-Belsen concentration camp. Weighing only fifty-five pounds and near death, I was liberated from that last camp on April 15, 1945.

After regaining my health, I worked in a displaced persons camp, where I helped organize the Jewish community. I also worked for organizations helping Holocaust survivors build new lives. After three years, I returned to Poland to attempt to regain lost family property and find out what I could about our family.

Because Poland was a communist country, the government had confiscated our family lands, and I was not permitted to leave the country after having gained admittance. Deciding to make the best of it, I returned to school and finished high school and college. I married my wonderful husband, Jacob Szapszewicz, and had two beautiful daughters, Rose and Joanne. I began to write articles for Polish magazines.

In 1959, we were granted permission to emigrate to the U.S., where I worked as a fashion advisor and manager of alterations in a department store and volunteered for the Jewish community. Since the opening of the Holocaust Museum and Learning Center in St. Louis, I have also worked there as a docent and lecturer. I continue to write articles and poetry for local and national publications.

I must take this opportunity to express my gratitude and appreciation to my late, beloved husband, Jacob Szapszewicz, for the many hours he spent listening to my poems, which I read aloud to him. He also told me stories from his youth, and I incorporated these stories into the pages of this book. I wish to thank my dear son-in-law, Gary Scott, for encouraging me to write my poems and stories, the early versions of some which he helped edit and print for me. I thank my wonderful, artistic daughter, Joanne, for her profound drawings, which add so much to my stories and poems. I thank my granddaughters, Marisa and Ariella Scott, for inspiring and proudly supporting me. I wish to express my deepest respect and gratitude to my editor, Dr. Robert Hutcheson, who is not only a great scholar but also a wonderful human being. I wish thankfully to acknowledge the countless hours he spent reading, correcting, and editing my poems and articles, as well as for organizing the material and doing everything else necessary to create this book. My thanks to Jim Murphy for the graphic design of the entire book and for the cover designs. Finally, I must express my deepest appreciation to Sue Jackson for her special role in my life.

My dear family and friends, this book would not be possible without you. Bob and Jim, thank you for caring so much about educating the world about the Holocaust and spending so much time and energy to ensure that it never happens again. I am so grateful to all of you for your contributions. I love you all with all my heart.

Maria Szapszewicz
St. Louis, Missouri

AN EDITOR'S REFLECTIONS:
MEMORY, POETRY, AND THE HOLOCAUST
An Address given 29 May 2003 at
Central Reform Congregation, St. Louis, MO

For several weeks, I've been strangely anxious about this evening's address because, in the midst of many possible avenues of approach to Maria's writings, I seemed unable to settle on a single aspect that would cohere into one integrated essay the various things I need to say.

Last Saturday evening, as I attended Mass at my parish church, during what would ordinarily have been the sermon, the pastor presented a helpful explanation of a relatively minor change in the order of worship: he discussed a respectful bow of the head which was to be introduced at several points in the liturgy. The pastor half-teasingly termed these bows of respect a type of "liturgical dance" but encouraged the congregation not to be intimidated; they wouldn't have to gyrate in any spectacular way. I began to reflect on this gentle sign and how suitable its use would be when approaching any member of creation, and not only those that we call human. Such a gesture might be a sort of a reminder and witness of one's sacred, holy value. By the end of Saturday's liturgy, I had recognized the handle and focus I was seeking, though I won't dwell on the mental itinerary that took me from ambiguity to relative clarity in speaking about Maria's poetry this evening.

In the past few decades, most of us have been touched in some way by the ravages of Alzheimer's disease. It seems a diabolic inversion of the plight of Odysseus' men under Kirke's spell who were turned into swine by her magic but who terrifyingly retained their human reason in this new, bestial body. The Alzheimer's victim, on the other hand, seems to lose his or her identity as the disease progresses until it seems there is a body without the person residing therein, so important is the personal human memory to our identification of ourselves as OUR SELVES.

Most likely, all of us treasure certain memories and perhaps have even established little personal rituals of recognition or remembrance. Of course, all of us tend to divide a great deal of our diurnal life up according to these remembrances. Let's look a bit at this blessing and this burden of memory.

As a teacher and student of English, I am immensely curious about word history. Let's examine several pertinent terms for a moment. The etymology of the word "memory," first of all, traces back to the equivalent of "mindful." However, its Indo-European base is curiously the ancestor of both remember and mourn. "To forget," on the other hand, comes from the Old English for "to miss your hold on"—there is a sort of grasping at nothing when we forget, an inability to find our place or our bearing. After my first bout with the editing of Maria's writings, I suggested a book title to her based on one of her poems. She, however, adamantly preferred to name the book *For The People I Love and Can't Forget*. She wanted to keep her bearings, to keep her hold on what she remembers and on those she particularly cherishes.

As I ponder what Maria includes in her poetry, I ask if there is anything here that she celebrates—a word that is associated with "attending a festival." Or is she a rebel—a word that plays with the Latin *bellum*, "war," and suggests that one is waging a war against one's conqueror. I believe Maria touches on all of these in her writing: remembrance and mourning, rebellion and accusation, lamentation and celebration. While most of our memories are appropriate to share in our home and local setting, there are some among us—like Maria—whose memories have a value beyond the local, beyond the private—they are of particularly humane, public, and global significance. Let's take a few moments now to reflect on some of what she has written.

In "The Home I Loved," and with nostalgia and idyllic memory, she treasures her and her husband's childhood, where

"Not too far from the forest, in the green valley
Next to the beautiful lake and flowing little stream,
Close to the water mill with the huge wooden wheel,

There stood a house
Built from stones and wood."

We are reminded here that poetry deals most often with the tangible—that which is made of stone and wood or which can be felt acutely in the pleasure or pain of the heart and spirit. She also depicts the house in this as the home that she loves, a site that retains part of her heart and spirit.

During the segment of her life which she and her mother spent—or perhaps lost--at Auschwitz, her vibrant memory was plagued by a different vision of the tangible. In "For Those Who Helped," she writes,s

"Oh, those too long nights in Auschwitz!
How I feared, how many times I wished my eyes would
be blurred!
But I could clearly see what was going on all about me."

Poets and prophets are privy to a great deal that is unsettling and difficult to bear, and poets and prophets often seem to forsake lives of normalcy and the so-called simple pleasures and burdens and responsibilities for a different calling. In "Memories from Auschwitz," Maria recalls in rhyming couplets a desire simply to endure, to survive, and to regain respect.

"My eyes are full of tears;
I am suffering; I am full of fears.
I pray and pray that I will survive this terrible pain.
And that some day I will be treated like a human being again."

All of us have most likely had our supper this evening, and each of us looks forward to a time to share food and to chatter freely after this program. This is not the norm in a concentration camp. In "Reflections from the Past," Maria writes,

"I recall how often I have heard from others,
Man does not live by bread alone.
Did they ever try to live without bread?"

Proverbial and biblical truisms take on here a new and bitter sense.

In the face of frequent deprivation and unmerited punishment, most people would be inclined to complain, as Job did, about the injustice of it all and, if they are believers, to ask the Almighty to explain and justify what is to the human reason largely inexplicable, as Countee Cullen did so eloquently in his sonnet "Yet Do I Marvel." Maria, a teenager at the time who should statistically have had no virulent disease and no profound cause for lament, tells us in a rhetorical question her sobering recognition of this horrendous status quo in "The Long Journey to Hell,"

"We knew we were going to die,
But still on our lips
Was the question, 'Why?'"

Almost sixty years after Liberation, Maria places these events and these memories in perspective. She does not summon us—"all men, women and children"—to join in a pilgrimage or a dance. In "I Am Accusing You," she wants us, instead, to understand.

"You, all men, women and children,
Come with me.
Let us take a long journey into the past.
Come on, all of you,
Let us leap back to the time
More than a half century ago.
For you, it is history;
For me, it is yesterday."

As many of you will know, the word "prophet" indicates in its etymology that one is speaking for another. In her prophetic passages, such as this one from "I Am Accusing You," Maria does not shy away from pointing the finger in an ultimate manner that, to me at least, is reminiscent of the Reproaches in the Holy Week liturgy of my own church. It is the wrongdoers who load the pallet of their victims with the gall of suffering and the bitterness of hopelessness.

> "Come on and look, all you,
> Both the murderers and the quiet bystanders.
> Behold what you have done.
> We must carry the heavy load of the memories
> Whose burden comes from you."

Maria makes us privy to those dark hours when so many human beings, even today in this community, may or will find falling asleep an impossible task because of extortion, hunger, imprisonment, pain, or guilt. For the survivor, as she writes in "The Last Remnants,"

> "It's so hard to deal with, and nobody understands.
> Only those who went through the long sleepless nights
> Understand the nightmares on the rare nights we are able to sleep."

How successful can the survivor of the Holocaust be—and one can, of course, be only a partial survivor: one who still daily feels the pangs of suffering from more than half a century ago—at dealing with a tormenting past, at eluding nightmares and daily mistrust, and at regaining some modicum of humanity, human respect, and love from and for another? Does time truly heal all wounds? Or is it fundamentally a matter of choice and practice? For Maria, in her poem "After Liberation,"

"... life was continuing its course.
We had to go on.
We realized we could not mourn forever.
They say time heals; time consoles.
But our memories and pain will last forever.
We cannot forget our loved ones. Never."

The patient benevolence of time and adequate stability of experience with loved ones and with those caring individuals outside our family can indeed help to heal some of this injury for some of us. "The Liberation" is jargon referring to an event for the multitude; but it identifies a profound and life-determining experience for survivors. I was not quite three years old when Maria and her beloved mother reached their Liberation on April 15, 1945. At that time, the two of them together weighed 101 pounds, not enough for the Red Cross to allow the two of them, weighed together, to donate a single pint of blood to our local blood bank. In "The Liberation," she remembers that

"It was a beautiful spring day;
You could feel it in the air.
The sun was shining bright—
It gave so much light!
Nature, after a long winter,
Came back to life.
The birds were singing,
The trees grew new little green leaves,
The grass was growing,
And it was the most beautiful day of my life."

These must surely be the words of a Maria in the future, not the words of the starved and disheveled twenty-year-old girl who needed nearly a full hour to stand up from a reclining position, so weak and undernourished was her body.

As we near an end to this brief reflection on Maria's poetic witness, let's return to a day in the idyllic adolescence of her dear husband Jacob. Like Simon, in **The Lord of the Flies**, Jacob, a man of immense intelligence and cultivation, had a secret hiding place where he could be by himself. In "The Hiding Place," Maria tells us about his secret haven many years ago.

> "It was not far away from our home and watermill;
> There was an immense hill
> Surrounded by tall and beautiful pine trees.
> On the top of the hill were large gray stones.
> No one paid attention to the hill;
> No one hiked to the summit or worked nearby.
> People just passed by as if it did not exist.
> Peasants they were, just minding their own business.
> Children were afraid to climb up the hill—
> There were terrible stories about the little mountain,
> But for me the hill was my hiding place.
> This was my Paradise.
> Here I was able to read my books;
> Nobody could see me to give me dirty looks
> As if I were wasting time, not working in the mine."

After hours of reading in this hiding place, Jacob lay down to take a bit of a snooze, awaking to find fiercely brewing storm clouds, and he quickly placed his precious book of the moment under a stone to keep it safe and dry. Recently, Jacob's sister found that book. It did survive, but in an utterly disintegrated condition, and, today, its contents can no longer be deciphered.

Can this be an allegory of the destined dilemma of poets like Maria who have survived the horrors, the memories, and the nightmares of the Holocaust? Are they "immense hills" of prophetic and testimonial experience to which no one pays attention and which everyone treats as if they do not exist? If that were true, insult would indeed have been added to the injury caused by the Nazi ideology, by the perpetrators who administered it, and by the bystanders who allowed it to function and thrive.

In another sylvan passage, Maria pens a kind of rewording of the dream-vision of Jacob in Genesis, wherein the Creator promises that Jacob will have descendants "as plentiful as the dust of the earth." In "We Jews," Maria, a child of this covenant, writes that

"We Jews are like the mushrooms in the woods.
After a terrible storm and heavy rain,
We come back, and not in vain."

We all know that Maria did in fact come back from her Journey into Hell, and—we also know—not in vain. The existence of her family, children, and grandchildren, and our presence in this sacred space tonight attest to that. Let's return to those several terms we examined just a few moments ago. In the presence of one another, we can remember, we can mourn and lament, we can pledge not to forget, and we can celebrate her survival and her faith. You bless and you inspire us, Maria, with the richness of your human gifts, and with your vivid memories and your prophetic utterances. May your literary descendants—your present and future readers—be as plentiful as the dust of the earth and as abundant as the mushrooms in the woods after a heavy rain.

Robert J. Hutcheson, Ph.D.
Mandel Fellow
U.S. Holocaust Memorial Museum

Maria Szapszewicz

POEMS
OF
THE
HOLOCAUST

FOR THE PEOPLE I LOVE AND CAN'T FORGET

THE HOME I LOVED

(Dedicated to my husband Jacob Szapszewicz)

Not too far from the forest, in the green valley
Next to the beautiful lake and flowing little stream,
Close to the water mill with the huge wooden wheel,
There stood a house
Built from stones and wood.
It looked like a painted picture.
This was my warm, sweet home.
This was where I grew up,
Grew up with pride and might,
And where I spent my youth.
Here I took delight in nature,
Which was for me the greatest adventure.
Here I watched the birds play and heard them sing,
And here the little ones first tried their wings.
Here, too, were my eyes almost blinded
By the beautiful colors of butterflies.
Here tiny boys were fishing and splashing their feet in the water.
Here the pigeons built their nests under the roof and fed their
      young,
And I watched them for hours.
I watched the chickens, geese and ducks hatching their eggs.
I longed to see the little ones break forth from their shells.
I loved to watch the cows with their ringing bells
And the shepherd playing a melody on his wooden pipe.
The dog chased the cats, and the squirrels climbed in the woods,
Always looking for their special foods.
The bees flew from one flower to another,
Gathering nectar for the queen and bringing it to the hives.
This was my world.
Why was it taken away from me, dear Lord?

FOR THOSE WHO HELPED

Oh, those too long nights in Auschwitz!
How I feared, how many times I wished my eyes would be blurred!
But I could clearly see what was going on all about me.
I looked through the window and saw
The red flames and the smoke issuing forth from the chimney,
Dancing a death dance in the dark night.
The sky became red and gray.
My heart and world were in such terrible pain;
No one, no one heard the innocents' pleas for life.
Where were you, you others, who let us suffer such a terrible fate?
We who are still alive wonder
What has become of our precious culture and civilization.
What happened?
Our wrath blames you for not standing up for justice.

But there were others—there were those who tried to help.
You tried to hide our identity,
You risked your own lives,
You were brave and righteous.
You made us believe that there were those who cared.
You made us aware that we were not alone,
That there were still good people in this world.
You did not forget the teaching of the Lord.
I shall always think of you with great love,
With gratitude and affection, so help me, dear G-d.

THE HIDING PLACE
(Dedicated to my husband Jacob)

It was not far away from our home and watermill;
There was an immense hill
Surrounded by tall and beautiful pine trees.
On the top of the hill were large gray stones.
No one paid attention to the hill;
No one hiked to the summit or worked nearby.
People just passed by as if it did not exist.
Peasants they were, just minding their own business.
Children were afraid to climb up the hill—
There were terrible stories about the little mountain,
But for me the hill was my hiding place.
This was my Paradise.
Here I was able to read my books;
Nobody could see me to give me dirty looks
As if I were wasting time, not working in the mine.
Here I could dream and listen to the birds chirp and sing
As they built their nests.
Here I could take a long rest;
This was the place I remember best.
From the top I could see, far away,
The beautiful green meadows and fields
And feel the light breeze
And see how the golden wheat bent back and forth.
Here I could see the rushing water from the streams,
And here I had the most beautiful dreams.
I read about distant lands and used my imagination
To envision a glorious world filled with wonderful people.

I did not realize that I knew so little,
Until one day, after reading for hours, I fell asleep.
And, when I awoke, I looked around at the gathering darkness,
The sky covered with dark clouds, the wind blowing so hard,
Swaying the branches of the trees.
No one was there except me.
I grew very frightened.
I placed the book under a stone so as not to get it wet.
I wanted it to be protected from the rain.
Then I looked down the slope,
And I could not believe what I saw:
The people of the village were carefully looking all around.
Some were even in little boats searching in the lake below.
My mother, father, brothers and sisters were running to and fro.
What happened? I wondered. What are they looking for?
Then I realized—they were looking for me.
I began to walk slowly down the hill.
I knew that my father would be very angry
That I created such a situation,
That the whole village was trying to find me.
They feared that I had drowned in the lake.
But here I am, all in one piece,
And so much awake!

Maria Szapszewicz

TODAY, NEVER TOMORROW

When you have work to do,
Don't wait; just do it now.
When you want to say something
Nice to a friend, say it now.
Don't wait for tomorrow.
Say it with love and compassion.
Today the sky is blue and bright,
And there is so much light.
Tomorrow the sky might be dark
And full of clouds.
If you are feeling blue and down,
Try to sing a song now.
Music will fill your heart
With love and compassion.

When you want to say
"I love you" to somebody,
Don't wait! Say it now;
Don't wait for tomorrow.
When you hurt someone,
Don't wait for fancy words to apologize.
Say "I'm sorry" now.
We are not here forever.
When you want to say
A kind word to somebody,
Don't put it off and wait for tomorrow.
Say it now.
Tomorrow may never come.
We all can make a better world today.
Never wait for tomorrow.

FRIENDSHIP

Friendship is one of the greatest treasures you can have.
It can't be counted or measured.
I once had a good friend.
We didn't ask much from each other.
Our friendship was expressed in great love and devotion.
There was, too, much unspoken emotion.
The world is such a complex place in which to live.
The horrible war that the Germans raged against us Jews
Pulled us in different directions.
We completely lost our connections.
Surviving the Holocaust,
I looked for him. The chances were very slim.
I couldn't find him.
I found out later that he was dead.
He was the only friend I had.
I cried and cried until I had no more tears.
My eyes became so dry,
But I didn't have any choice.
I had to go on with my life.
Time eased my tension and pain.
You can't mourn forever,
Though tragedies like this should happen never.
I prayed to G-d for peace,
So my pain would be released.

THE WARSAW GHETTO

There are so many people
Fenced within such a small place . . .
Just because of their race?
The streets are very crowded.
The people and children are walking.
You can see people crying.
Some of them are praying,
Others are dying.
Some are already dead
And lie on the sidewalks.
It is so heart-wrenching.
The children are stretching out their hands
And begging for bread.
There are others selling homemade cigarettes.
The deprived youth are suffering from malnutrition.
They are cold and wear torn clothes.
Their faces are milky white, and they have toothpick legs.
Immense flies buzz over their heads.
Those children's eyes were full of
Pain and bewilderment.
Those large eyes were accusing,
As the people of the world stood by idly
And acted so indifferent.
Not wishing to stop the massacre of guiltless victims,
They simply blocked their eyes and ears.
They didn't want to stop the Germans' cruelty.
They let the Jews die in vain because
Those bystanders themselves were not in pain.
There were other young people in the ghetto

Who started to revolt.
It was excruciatingly difficult to counter
The Germans' might.
The Jews felt strongly that their battle was already lost.
They would much rather fight and die in dignity
Than be led like sheep to the slaughter.
This was the ghetto where thousands of Jews
Perished in vain.
This terrible tragedy will leave on the
Germans' world a lasting stain.
May such a calamity never happen again.

A LONG WAY TO AUSCHWITZ

So many cattle cars wait for us on the ramp;
On each of us is a "Jude" stamp.
We walked so slowly to those marked cars,
Most of us praying aloud.
Some of us were begging G-d for mercy;
Many were spared the humiliation—
They were dying from starvation.
I was walking and talking to my dear mother;
We were separated from our father and brothers.
I pleaded with her;
I asked her not to give up hope.
We were sitting or standing in the cars,
Packed inside them; there was so little space.
It was such a horrible disgrace
To keep people under such duress.
Why were the Germans so obsessed?
We had no air; it was suffocating.
We were so terribly intimidated.
For this was everything so calculated.

I tried to look through the cracks.
It was harvest time.
I saw some peasants driving through,
Their carts loaded with bags of cabbage.
They were trying to help;
They threw cabbage leaves toward us.
That was indeed a risky task.
Although we couldn't reach for the leaves,
Those people had compassion.
They stopped throwing,
They crossed themselves and prayed.
We were in such despair,

But this encouragement made us feel better.
There were still those who cared.
My heart and soul were so badly bruised.
Then I said to myself, "I will never be defeated
By the way I am treated,
And, by G-d's will, I will overcome this terrible ordeal.
I will tell the world what happened to our sisters and brothers,
Children, mothers and fathers."

Maria Szapszewicz

MEMORIES FROM AUSCHWITZ

My heart is full of pain;
That is why I am writing again.
The world is full of dark mud;
I cannot understand why they had to spill our blood.
Why did they turn into cruel animals?
In spite of their culture and civilization.
They wanted to lead us to annihilation.
"Why? And why?" is always on my lips.
Their hearts are so cold and full of hate;
Why do we Jews have to be their bait?
I look and see that once again come the trains;
The blood is freezing in my veins.
Oh, my G-d, there are so many people suffering and in pain!
They are crying and praying for the oncoming day.
It is growing very dark;
Only the sky is full of flashing flames.
Why did they turn into animal hordes?
For this there are not adequate words.
My eyes are full of tears;
I am suffering; I am full of fears.
I pray and pray that I will survive this terrible pain.
And that some day I will be treated like a human being again.

Memories and Dreams

Sitting in the dirty barrack,
Full of exhausted, half-dead people,
And looking out through the windows,
Seeing how the smoke and fire exploded from the chimney,
I try hard not to think,
But I can't help it,
Imagining whose body burns in the flames.
My G-d, I am full of fears.
Who is going to be next?
Looking, trying to push away the terrible scene,
I think, "How could this happen?"
Yet the world is so beautiful,
The sky so blue,
And the sun so bright,
Sending the golden rays to make light and warm the earth,
And all of a sudden I feel a little better.
A small spark of hope gives me comfort and breaks my sorrow,
And I start to pray to G-d for a better tomorrow.

REFLECTIONS FROM THE PAST

Oh, those memories and terrible dreams!
How I wish I could push them away,
Far away into the back of my head.
I wake up; I am still in bed.
Bitter memories of my youth,
Many times have I wished to erase them,
But they always return.
They haunt me; they chase me.
Where can I run? What can I do?

I recall how often I have heard from others,
Man does not live by bread alone.
Did they ever try to live without bread?
Unless one is starved to death,
No one will ever understand,
Only those who shared my fate in those tragic days
When civilization and humanity were also put to death.

For Those Innocent
People I Loved

My heart is crying
For those who are dying.
My heart is crying
For the children who are dying.
Not knowing what it means to be dead,
They are marching to the gas chambers,
Holding high their heads.
My heart is crying
For their mothers and fathers;
Holding onto their children tight,
They know the Germans' might.
Even so, some of them try to fight.
My heart is crying,
O dear G-d, why do You not hear our cry?

My eyes are growing dry.
The sky is brilliant red,
And everybody around me is dead.
I cry and cry, and I want to know
Why our chosen people had to die,
And my heart will always cry
Until the day when I, too, shall die.

THE TREE AND ME
(Dedicated to my husband Jacob)

Next to our house grew a large tree
With huge, spreading branches.
This tree knew so many secrets!
If only it could talk!
Everybody so much loved that tree,
Especially me.
I was always reading books under it
And looking at the beautiful blue sky,
Listening to the songs of the birds
Who were always flying in big flocks,
Enjoying the light breeze
And watching the leaves move back and forth.

This tree gave shade and shelter to so many people.
Children were playing all kinds of games,
Calling each other funny names.
Others sat under the branches,
Resting on hot days.
They talked, joked and gossiped in their own ways.
This tree listened to everybody
But never could talk.

And when the fall and winter came
And the weather turned cold,
The leaves would turn yellow and fall off the branches,
Covering the earth.
Then I could no longer sit beneath the tree.
I was so sad and unhappy looking at the naked branches,
Sometimes covered with snow.
I really didn't know—
I thought that the cold weather would last forever.
But finally the sun shone bright again,
Warming up the world.

I was so grateful to the Lord
That we had spring again.

The tree came back to life.
After a long winter came little buds and twigs
Which turned to small green leaves and flowers.
How fragrant was the perfume!
Soon I would be able to sit or sleep beneath the tree
And dream, dream about all sorts of things,
And make wishes!
If only I had wings
And could be strong and tall as the tree
And could fly up to the top
And see the beautiful world—
The valleys, rivers, woods and streams,
The golden wheat bending under the breeze!

Such was my dream.
This was a fantasy
Of a young boy like me.

THE LONELY TREE

The forest was burning fast,
And people didn't want to
Or couldn't stop watching the flames.
Birds were flying back and forth
Trying frantically to protect their offspring
And save their nests.
The disoriented animals were scattering,
But they couldn't escape the wooden inferno
Whose flames climbed high in the sky.
A true fiery blanket encircled the forest
And embraced the trees.
Alone amidst this scene
Stood one tree, darkened by the smoke,
Its branches broken but its roots firmly planted.
This lonely tree had been planted for me by my parents.
Now it had only a few twigs left,
And everyone thought it was dead, like the others.
When spring arrived, however,
The tree came back to life and started to grow.
Little branches began to show, along with
A few buds which promised to transform into leaves.
This wondrous little tree was itself,
And this tree was me.

Maria Szapszewicz

THE LONG JOURNEY TO HELL

Five very long days,
Four nights even longer,
Sitting in a closed cattle car,
Hungry, thirsty, dehumanized,
Humiliated, degenerated,
Stripped of humanity and dignity,
With no food or water,
Lying on dirty, contaminated floors.
The Germans had no remorse.
Some of us were crying,
Some were dying.
Some were so ill with fever,
Some were laughing—not from happiness,
But from bewilderment.
Against their own will,
Their voices sounded like terrible shrieks.
Others were praying and dreaming
About a good world,
Asking, "Why, dear Lord,
Is this happening?"
Some were looking through the window cracks,
While others behind were pulling at their backs
Everyone wanted to see
The beautiful green fields and meadows,
The rolling hills, the innocent blue sky,
The sun shining bright.
On everyone's lips was the question, "Why?"
The wheels of the trains rolled so slow,
And our spirits were unbelievably low.
We had lost our hope and determination;
We were giving up without hesitation.
We knew we were going to die,
But still on our lips
Was the question, "Why?"

FOR MY MOTHER

The night in the camp is so dark and long;
We are starving, we are cold.
I was sleeping next to the window,
Watching the smoke rise from the chimney.
The wind blew fiercely, scattering the red flames.
I recalled my perished friends' names.
They are not here anymore.
To think so was not wise,
Yet I prayed that they had awoken in Paradise.
I was so scared. I looked for my dear mother.
Then one girl said, "Don't bother."
But I found her, not far away.
I cared so much for her—
It was she who gave me so much love and inspiration.
I was so lucky having her and receiving her determination.
She it was who always said to me,
"Be strong. Have courage, my child."
The Germans are wild,
Malicious and vicious—
Thirsty for Jewish blood.
What made them hate us so much?
Other people are indifferent;
They don't want to stand for us.
But we have to survive—this is a "must."
I said, "Mom, I am still hungry and cold."
She kissed me, hugged me,
And took me in her arms.
"Come close to me, my dear child.
We will warm each other with our bodies.
We will fall asleep and dream of a better world
Where you will no longer be hungry and cold."

FOR THE UNKNOWN JEWISH PARTISAN

(To my dear and brave husband Jacob)

You men, women and children,
You, who fought in the forests, meadows, fields and sky;
You who had such great courage to resist the German might,
You who did not even know how to fight;
You knew that you were fighting a losing battle,
Like a fly fighting an elephant.
You would rather die with honor and dignity
Than be led like sheep to the slaughter.
You fought for our liberty, all of you, young and old,
Fighters of the ghettoes and camps.
You women, carriers and smugglers of armaments and ammunition,
Often hauling them through the sewers, choking from the foul odor,
Your bodies wet from the contaminated water.
Nobody knows your names.
You acted from your own free will and determination.
You wanted to save the Jewish nation.
You quiet heroes—how often mounted your disgust
That the people of the world could be so unjust.
Why could not more of them have stood up for us
As the earth was soaked with our blood?
Scattered are your bones and ashes.
You were the most precious flowers of your nation.
You fought for us without hesitation,
Your lives cut short by the Germans.
Most of you did not live long enough to see the liberation,
But we will always remember you with great love and devotion.
May we also fight for a better tomorrow,
So that nobody should experience again such a terrible sorrow.

Our Mill
(To my dear husband)

I loved the flour mill with the huge water wheel.
Sitting in a boat and dreaming about a beautiful world,
I loved the great lake.
I loved the big tree with the large branches growing next to our
     house.
I can still hear the birds singing.
I see the flock of geese walking and pecking.
I see the dog chasing the cat, which sometimes made me mad.
I see the dog following me to school.
Everything is gone.
Where have those days gone?
Is everything vanished? Is all vanity?
I surely missed my train.
I am here. I survived this horrible time.
Where is my family, which I loved so much?
They will always be in my mind.
For them, there is no mill and there is no house.
I am here to tell you the sad story, a story without glory,
The great pain which will last forever
Because I will see my family in this world never.

Maria Szapszewicz

THE SHTETL

Forever gone are those people:
A shoemaker who was a mentor,
A tailor who was a cantor,
The barber who was a healer,
A joiner who was a shammash,
A rabbi who was a judge
(And you had to obey him—
This was a "must").
The little girls were growing so fast,
They had no say or will
When their parents struck a deal with the matchmaker!
Gone are the Jewish schools called cheders,
Where the boys studied Torah-gemorah.
Gone are the great painters,
Cantors, poets, writers, and scientists.
Most of them perished,
But their work did not vanish.
It will live forever, enriching our lives,
And we shall forget them never.
Gone are the people of the shtetl,
Gone are their homes and possessions.

Also gone is their cemetery.
The people of the town would not even let
The dead rest in peace.
They took the headstones away from the graves.
With them they paved the roads and paths to their homes,
And they let the grass grow tall and wild.
The sun is high, shining bright,
And the wind is blowing the leaves so mild.
The cattle and goats graze among the graves.

Whoever would expect from a neighbor such a disgrace?
We who have so much respect for others,
We who contributed so much to civilization,
We survivors will not go away.
We are here to stay.
We build new lives.
We now have our own country.
This is the most wonderful bounty.
We will always be the world's eternal light.
Thanks to G-d, we have the will and might.

WE JEWS

We Jews are such a distinct tribe;
We Jews are the chosen people.
Chosen for what? To suffer and be scattered?
So many times in the camps, I heard others ask,
Why has the Almighty chosen us?
Could He not choose others?
We, the Jewish people,
Learn so little from others.
We who were gassed, burned,
Starved to death, hanged,
Persecuted, tortured,
Will there be an end to it?
Can we use our wits?

We are determined to survive.
We survived the Holocaust, the greatest tragedy
Perpetrated against us.
There were those who wished to bring us to annihilation,
But some of us had great determination
To live and tell our stories.
We Jews are like the mushrooms in the woods.
After a terrible storm and heavy rain,
We come back, and not in vain.
We grow and grow better and more numerous,
Even though we have been dispersed
And locked in ghettoes.
We always had to do it on our own;
Too few wanted to help us.
Did it ever dawn on others
That we, too, have our dignity?
We always believed in liberty.

There is only one way if life for all of us to survive:
We have our Torah, the most precious gift.
We try to live by the commandments;
Only G-d can judge us.
We now have our own country,
And we want every human being to live free.
All the people of the world
Should live by these simple rules.

They Left the Shoes

Wherever you look
You see shoes,
Piles and mountains of shoes.
Some of them were once squeaking;
They were almost brand new.
Some had holes and leaked.
Some shoes were beautifully polished
And some were completely demolished.
Shoes of almost all colors
And shoes of all sizes—
Narrow, wide, bright, light, tight.
Shoes with high heels;
Shoes with low heels.
Shoes for display.
Shoes with nails.
Some even had skates.
And some were single,
Without a mate.
Shoes very fancy,
With beautiful bows.
Some were so worn out,
They were patched.
Some didn't match.
Some shoes had laces.
There were even shoes with braces.
Other shoes had beautiful good looks.
There were men's shoes, women's shoes,
Children's shoes, and even babies' shoes.
These shoes were worn by people
To walk, to run, to kick.
Some were for happy occasions,
Some for sad.

When I looked at them,
I became very angry.
Those babies' shoes,
Those poor babies' shoes
In which babies tried to take
Their first steps,
In which they tried
To learn to walk
And did take a few steps
Before falling into their mothers' laps.
Those fancy shoes worn by women
Who walked with such grace.
And I can see each face.
Shoes and shoes and shoes--
Where are all the people
Who wore those shoes?
What a terrible shame
That there is nobody to claim
Those shoes.
And we all know
Who is to blame.
Yes, those shoes belonged
To our mothers, fathers, sisters, and brothers,
And to our children.
What is left of those piles of shoes
Can't talk. Their masters are dead.
This is what happened,
And it is really very sad.

Maria Szapszewicz

THE HANDS

The hands are very
Important parts of our bodies.
They can do good things
For people and bad.
But what I have to tell you
Is more than sad.

There are hands that are so gentle,
So fragile, so soothing,
Hands caressing,
Hands touching, hands accusing.
There are hands that are healing,
Hands working hard to
Make a living,
Hands expressing their love,
Hands stretching out to others,
Hands praying, hands blessing,
Hands giving so much to others,
Hands beating up others,
Hands pinching,
Hands lynching,
Unpitying hands choking people to death.

Oh, my dear folks,
You know so little about
What those beasts did to us
With their dirty hands,
Smeared with our blood.
You didn't, you wouldn't
Listen to us when we tried

To open our wounds and
Our broken hearts to tell you
About this, our terrible tragedy.
Now you are awake, and we are still talking
Because we have to.
The world must know
What the hands of the Nazis did to us.

WHERE WERE YOU?

I am free, but I do not really know what to do with myself,
Looking around and thinking about this horrible catastrophe.
Why did the Germans do this to us?
What drove them mad so they lost their humanity and heart?
Where was their culture and civilization?
Why did they lose their compassion, love and respect for others?
Did they believe in G-d and his religion;
Did they have any guilt or vision?
How can one person poison so many minds
And inspire them commit such terrible crimes?
Still can I see and hear the moaning of the dying,
I can hear the whispering of the "Shema Yisrael" on their lips.
Why didn't you people stand up for us?
Why were you so unjust?
Oh men, oh men, G-d's pure creations!
These are not false allegations.
Never shall I comprehend the Nazis' motivation
To put our mothers, fathers and children to death.
So I blame you men for being indifferent,
Not even thinking of blinking your eye
At the greatest tragedy in the world—such a crime!
Never forget, men,
You are not without heart or soul.
You will pay for this.
It will haunt you all your life,
Whatever you do, whatever you try.

THE CRIMES OF THE WORLD

The heavens are crying, and so few care
That we Jews are dying.
The whole sky is covered with clouds,
Which hang so low over the earth.
Only the sun is red, like a huge fireball.
There is fire, fire wherever you look.
It erupts from the crematorium chimney.
It is mixed with black smoke,
While the wind blows it in my direction.
The flames are so low that I can scarcely breathe.
I choke; there is no air.
I cry. I want to run away,
But there is no place to escape.
I am so frightened that I cover my head with my hands.
I am scared that the sparks will catch my hair,
Whatever is left of it.
My hands burn from the heat.

There is no place to go.
I am fenced in, locked in,
Like a wild animal in a cage.
Oh, my dear G-d, what a horrible place!
On the other side of the fence lies a beautiful world
Where people are free.
Why? We Jews couldn't fit into this world.
We were singled out to die.
Why does the world commit such a crime?
What have we done to deserve such degradation,
We who have suffered for generations,

Who have stood up for others when so few cared?
We are small in numbers among the nations
But rich in spirit and determination.
We would reach and embrace the world
With our love for peace,
Not asking for praise or admiration.
We would build a better world
For our children and for future generations
With the help of our dear Lord.

I Am Accusing You

You, all men, women and children,
Come with me.
Let us take a long journey into the past.
Come on, all of you,
Let us leap back to the time
More than a half century ago.
For you, it is history;
For me, it is yesterday.

I cannot forget those who were sisters, brothers,
Mothers, fathers and, above all, children.
Never does a day pass where I do not think of them.
They are inscribed deep in my heart.
I see them arising from my soul,
Marching, tired from the long exhausting trip,
Walking to their deaths,
Yet with hope and prayer on their lips.
I hear them reciting the shema.
How could I ever forget my dear, innocent people?

Those images torment me
Even at night when I lie in bed;
I cannot part from them,
And I am driven mad.
Everything returns to my mind;
I awaken from tormented dreams,
Sweating and in pain, and I start to scream.
Then I realize that this was a dream, all in the past:
A nightmare.

Oh, those nights, those horrible nights.
Why can I not forget and live like others,
Surrounded by the family I love?

Come on and look, all you,
Both the murderers and the quiet bystanders.
Behold what you have done.
We must carry the heavy load of the memories
Whose burden comes from you.

But in spite of everything, we have rebuilt our lives;
We have instilled in our children great love and,
Above all, hope for a better tomorrow.
Some day the world will be a better, safer place to live;
People will live in peace, they will respect one another.
And we will live in dignity.

THE DENIERS OF THE HOLOCAUST

You people asking me a question,
Who are those deniers?
I will tell you as a survivor.
They are the worst liars.
They are the ones who want to
Destroy Holocaust history.
It's for me an unbelievable mystery,
How they hate and discriminate.
Their hands are still wet from the Jews' blood.
Why don't you remove the blinders from your eyes?
We won't forget our loved ones
And what you have done to them.
A day doesn't go by that we don't cry
Till our eyes become dry.
We can't stop grieving.

Being a survivor is believing in a better world.
We suffered so much because you were full of hate.
Remember, we Jews will no longer be your bait.
We survivors are still alive.
We will fight you with all our might.
We are strong, and killing people is wrong.
Education is our weapon.
You lie out of desperation.
We can't understand what you gain by
Denying the Holocaust.

You are the ones who are losing your face.
As dignified humans, you've lost your place.
Soon will come your day.
You will go to Hell. I know this very well,
That lying and stealing are deceiving.
You are saying the Holocaust is not true.
The truth will never be the same for me and you.

FOR MINDY

It doesn't matter
What the world
Will do or say.
My heart still aches
The same way.

I can't sleep like others,
Free from pain.
The terrible memories
From the past
Bother me so much.
I put my faith in you
Because you were the only one
Who helped me.

You, who let me live
When the terrible
Winds were blowing
And they scattered
The dark smoke mixed
With fire coming out
Of the crematorium chimneys.

I heard the people crying
When they were dying.
I heard them begging for mercy,
Tightly holding onto their children.
The people of the world were
So indifferent.
They did not want to help the victims.

They let them die in vain
Because
They themselves were not in pain.
Their hideous crime will leave
An everlasting stain.

Maybe those indifferent people
Will learn a lesson:
Not to let atrocities like the
Holocaust happen again.

For My Brothers

How vividly I remember you both.
I can still see you laughing, talking, and playing games.
I dream about you often, and, when I close my eyes,
I want those dreams to last forever.
Although I know that I will never see you again,
As long as I live, you will live in my memory.
You are inscribed in my heart and soul with the power of love.

It will always be a puzzle for me. I can't understand why the
Germans had so much hate in their hearts as
They killed, starved, and gassed completely innocent people.
Had they completely lost their faith in G-d?
They caused so much pain,
And they made us suffer in vain
While the world quietly stood by.
Far too few tried to stop the killing
Of the innocent victims of the German madness.

FOR MY DEAR HUSBAND

I am almost always full of grief.
I always wanted to live,
And I knew in my heart that evil cannot finally succeed.
Although I have survived this terrible ordeal,
There isn't a day that I am not in terrible pain.
I still struggle and fight with all my strength to go on,
And life is not an easy task.
You must adjust to everything so fast.

Now, when I am old, I am grateful to G-d
That I am still alive.
But it is very hard to see one's loved one
Fade away day by day.
I know that soon we will have to part.
To think about this breaks my heart.
I pray and pray that G-d first takes me away.
I won't be able to overcome this unbelievable pain.
I know better than anybody the meaning of life.
I believe that the body is dying,
But everybody's soul keeps on flying.

MY OWN HOUSE OF PRAYER

In the corner of my heart and soul,
I have my own little prayer house
Where I pray during the day and,
Sometimes too, during sleepless nights.
When I open my eyes, I start to cry
For those who were chosen to die,
And I ask our dear Lord:
Why do people have in them such malice,
Such injustice and viciousness?
Why do they want to kill and torture others?
These thoughts overwhelm me.
I feel a terrible pain in my heart,
And I start to choke.
I can still see and smell the vivid smoke,
And I do not know if I am still awake.
I start to pray then for a better world:
My dearest Lord, transform it soon.

Maria Szapszewicz

AFTER LIBERATION

What will the next day bring after we are set free—
Still exhausted from a long time of starvation
But enjoying the freedom at last,
Not suffering from humiliation and deprivation?

We had to find the courage to go on with our lives.
We had to fit into this world which seems an alien mold.
Our hearts and souls were so badly bruised;
We were still licking our bleeding wounds,
And, like children when they started to learn how to walk,
We began to think and talk.
We looked around and realized we were left alone.
We had lost our loved ones,
Mothers, fathers, sisters, brothers, whole families.
Gone were our houses and possessions.
We had seen our chances grow dim.

Some of us felt great guilt,
But we tried to build new lives.
We had the drive and knew we must survive.
We were under horrible stress;
Our minds went wild, our thoughts flew so fast.
People living normal lives couldn't even guess.
We realized how hard it is to live alone
When everything had vanished,
When almost an entire race had perished.
Some of us lost the will to survive,
And most of us were very depressed
Under such terrible stress.

We started more and more to feel the pain;
We had lived a long time in vain.

But life was continuing its course.
We had to go on.
We realized we could not mourn forever.
They say time heals; time consoles.
But our memories and pain will last forever.
We cannot forget our loved ones. Never.

THE WORKING CHILDREN OF THE GHETTO

They come from all sides, like the water of little streams
That flows into the oceans.
Their faces are without emotions.
They look like the old.
They have lifeless, turgid eyes.
Their gaze reaches far away.
They see a spark of light.
They try to live in a different world,
Where there is plenty food, where life is safe and good,
Where the sun shines bright to warm their cold bodies,
Where the grass is green
And the sky is blue and cloudless
And the trees reach such a height
That no one fears the Germans' might.
The trees are laden with fruit,
And they the children will dance and play, happy and gay.

But soon they stop dreaming;
They have to face the harshness of reality.
The gates of the workshops open,
And the children are incarcerated inside.
They toil away beneath the guard's watchful eyes.
"Work, work, you dirty little Jews!"
Swollen are their legs, haggard their bodies.
Oh, those poor children of the ghetto,
They cannot understand
Why there is so much hate in this world.
Can You answer them, dear Lord?

The Birds

After a long, long winter,
The spring arrived.
We looked forward
To warmer weather
And to much longer days.
The sky shone a beautiful blue,
With only a few white floating clouds
Looking as if they would
Chase each other and disappear.
The trees were releasing little buds,
And the sun shone bright,
Letting out golden rays.
But we were hungry, starving.
We couldn't walk
And had to crawl out of the barracks.
For some of us, it was even hard to talk.
Yet we wanted to warm up our frozen bodies.
We couldn't even sit.
Crawling on our hands and feet,
We looked like animals.
We didn't believe we would have another chance
To enjoy more sunny days.
We were sitting, trying to hold up our heads.
Then we heard a very loud noise and
Couldn't believe our eyes.
Birds were flying in large flocks,
So many of them.
Circling, cackling, spreading their wings.

Those birds were flying so very high—
They would cry,
For they were afraid to die.
They couldn't find any food, for everything was bare.
And we couldn't share; we were starved.
I wished and prayed, why couldn't I be a bird—
To fly away and be free like them.

Our Lost Children

Children, children. Joske, Shmulke, Srulke,
Chajkes, Surkes, Malkes and Esterkes.
Playing in the small courtyards
Of their apartment buildings,
They couldn't see a tree or grass.
They were playing all kinds of games.
Those were the very happy days.
The children had so much energy and were so full of life.
They were playing, some barefoot,
Some of them with runny noses.
Some had torn clothes.

Oh, my dear little ones,
Your laughter still rings in my ears—
Your great joy of life
And your drive to survive.
You know that you can always come home
Where your mother will feed you bread and hot soup.
Your parents always did the best they could;
They were poor in money but rich in spirit.
They gave their children warmth, love and inspiration.
Those children grew with no feeling of deprivation.
This helped them to get their proper education.
But where are those children now?
As grownups, they would have given so much to civilization!
The sky is so beautiful and blue,
And the sun shines so bright.
The trees flower, and the grass is green
And grows so mild.

But brutish persons went wild
And put our children to death.
Empty are those courtyards;
We will never hear our children's happy voices.
Forever are gone those cheerful noises.
I shall never forget your smiling faces.
You are inscribed on my heart and soul
With love and greatness.

Children, children. Joske, Shmulke, Srulke,
Chajkes, Surkes, Malkes and Esterkes.
They once played in the small courtyards
Of their apartment buildings.
And there were a million and a half of them.

THE EYES

There are all kinds of eyes,
And they have many colors—
Blue, green, hazel, gray brown.
There are even evil eyes.
The colors can be so beautiful;
The eyes can have all kinds of shapes.
They can be so powerful.
The eyes are the windows
Of the human body, of the soul,
And they have all kinds of expression.
Most of the time, our eyes
Can speak more than words.

So many German eyes were full of hate.
I have seen their eyes; most of them were red.
They could kill you dead.
They had no feeling, emotion, nor compassion.
Those eyes were devil eyes—
So sick, so red, so full of hate,
Always looking for the bait,
The defenseless, poor Jew,
To butt and to beat.
The Jews were the scapegoats,
The innocent victims
Of the Germans' madness.
There was such a terrible sadness.
I witnessed the horrors with my own eyes:
The mothers, the fathers, and the children,
Marching to the valley of the dead,
Their eyes flowing with pain.

There were also eyes that never gave up hope.
There were many wise eyes,
Eyes begging for mercy.
There were eyes full of warmth, love and compassion.
Others full of resignation—
Eyes looking high up in the sky,
Proud and praying loud.

Eyes crying and eyes dying—
I have seen them; they were everywhere.
Eyes, eyes, and eyes.
I have seen them; there were so many.
And where were the eyes of the rest of the world?
Those eyes were cold and so indifferent.
They were without emotion.
They would not act to save
And help the victims' eyes.
They let them die in vain.
Nobody was opposing those hateful eyes.
They let them commit the worst crimes in human history.
But where were the other people's eyes?
This is for me an inscrutable mystery.

Eyes crying and eyes dying—
I have seen them; they were everywhere.
Eyes, eyes, and eyes.
There were some eyes that were healing,
But most of them were killing.

JANUS KORCZAK
(Dedicated to Lolle Boettcher for her devotion to humanity
and her efforts to help people live together in peace and dignity)

Janusz Korczak,
The man who loved children.
G-d made the world a beautiful place to live,
The sun shining bright, giving so much
Warmth and light to the earth,
Trees growing tall,
Grass green, flowers blooming with beautiful colors,
Rivers and streams flowing wildly,
Oceans roaring, birds singing, bees buzzing.
G-d made people like you.

Janusz Korczak was a doctor
Who respected children's bodies and souls.
He wanted them to have a home,
Not to be alone.
He believed in the children,
Who are the world's future.
He was a man so loving and kind,
He could read the child's mind,
Children with all kinds of faces.
He accepted them without conditions,
This was his life's mission.
He was the first one to stand up for their rights
And to treat them with great dignity,
Regardless of their ability.

They trusted him
He defended them against abuse and humiliation.
He had for them so much love and admiration.
He taught them right from wrong,

And those children grew up without deprivation.
He helped them to get a good education.
Those poor children had been hungry;
They had lived in the ghetto
Where there was horrible starvation.
He told them to believe in a bright future
Where there would be no sorrow,
Where people would live together in respect and tolerance.

Janusz Korczak believed in liberty.
The children asked him why
The world had closed its ears and eyes.
Why don't they hear our cries?
But the Germans' bloody eyes were cold
And their hearts were hard as steel.
They murdered our children, young and old.
Those children were the flowers of our nation.
Janusz Korczak marched alongside these children
To the cattle cars, their heads held high.
Hateful, murderous Germans
Put our children to death.

Janusz Korczak was and is a hero of our nation
Because of his love of children and humanity.
He put to shame the uncaring culture and indifferent civilization.
Janusz Korczak truly deserves our respect and admiration.

DREAMS

Some nights I dream that I am a child.
I am at home with my family,
Surrounded with love and warmth
From my dear mother, my father and brothers.
I play all kinds of games with my brothers.
All of a sudden I realize that I am alone.
I start to cry and to yell:
Don't leave me alone by myself.
I am scared of others; I feel that they
Are going to take me away.
I see the ghosts emerging from the chimney's fire.
They dance a dance of death.
I start to cry. It all doesn't make any sense.
But I cry, and my eyes flood with tears.
Nobody hears my crying except the earth.

DON'T DESPAIR

I had great faith
I had many plans
I had hope
I had such love
In my heart
I had striven
And had my best given
My heart and soul
Was completely broken
Until one day
I was awoken
That day, I heard a voice

It was my dearest mother
Don't give up, my dear child
Resist and fight
The Germans' might
Look at the innocent blue sky
See the sun shining bright
Dream about a good world
Where people live
By G-d's word
Push forward as hard
As you can do
Then your dreams
Will come through

Remember, my dear child
There is always a new day
So called a tomorrow
Which will heal
Your wounds and sorrow
This will be for you
A new beginning
With our dear Lord willing

My Beliefs

I believe in the human mind.
I believe in miracles and G-d's blessings.
I believe in human abilities.
I believe not everybody hates.
I believe there are some people who
Have love in their hearts, and
They are able to do good things for others.
I believe that people should accept people.
I believe that people should not discriminate against any others.
I believe that we are all G-d's creation.
I believe, therefore, that we should live in peace
And respect others even if their faith is not ours.
I believe we all can make a better world where G-d is Lord.
I believe people can live in peace and dignity.
I believe that this will happen.
Above all, I believe in you, dear G-d,
Who saved me from the evil claws.
I survived a terrible ordeal
In a world where humanity and civilization both died,
Where people stopped being human beings
And turned into beasts.
I continue to believe that people always have
Something good to give
And are called to make this world a better place.

MUSIC AND SONGS

They saved my life.
Music is something that you can hear,
Something you can make up.
This also holds for a song.
You can play it
And enjoy it.
You can sing
And join others.
You don't have to understand it all.
Music and songs express
Your feelings.
When you listen,
They take a hold of you.
They take over
Your whole body and soul.
It will heal your mind;
It will touch your bleeding heart.
With great emotion,
It will bring up your spirit
And your love of life.
When we in the camps
Tried so hard to strive,
Songs and music
Brought serenity and peace.
It was songs and music
That helped me so much to survive
During the darkest days of my shattered life.
It is so remarkable,
It is almost unbelievable,
That some people
Had this G-d-given gift
And made up songs in the camp—
Beautiful melodies and lyrics.
Their bodies were weak from starvation,

Their spirits high in inspiration.
The songs which healed their souls and minds
Helped them survive the hunger and
humiliation.

I shall never forget,
I will always remember,
The Italian girls singing
Loud the song "Mama."
Such beautiful voices
And such emotion in those songs, so much pain.
Those songs ring in my ears.
With those songs, they went to death.
But we will remember them;
They are in our hearts forever.
As long as we will live,
They will live too.

THE LIBERATION

It was a beautiful spring day;
You could feel it in the air.
The sun was shining bright—
It gave so much light!
Nature, after a long winter,
Came back to life.
The birds were singing,
The trees grew new little green leaves,
The grass was growing,
And it was the most beautiful day of my life.

I regained my liberty and my dignity.
I was sick and weak, hungry,
Starved almost to death.
And, suddenly, I became angry and mad.
I looked around to find some of my friends,
But almost all of them were dead.
I touched my mother;
She did not respond.
I started to cry, "Mom, Mom, we are free!
Please, why don't you talk to me?"
I was scared that I had lost her.
But, all of a sudden,
She opened up her beautiful blue eyes.
"Dear child, what did you say?"
'Mom, Mom, we are free,
You and I and all the others?"
And she said, "What about your father
And my two sons, your brothers?"

I cried and said, "Mom, I want you to live.
You have so much to give,
You who always taught me never to give up,
To be strong and live with determination.
This is not an exaggeration.
Mom, Mom, look outside;
It is a beautiful world.
Now we will have enough food.
I hope the people will be good.
We will be an example for future generations.
We Jews have a secret weapon—
Our Torah. We believe in education.
No one will bring us to annihilation.
We will carry the burning torch.
We will ignite the whole world.
So help us, O dear Lord."

The Cemetery

Thinking I might find my ancestors' graves,
I went to the cemetery,
But I was unpleaseantly surprised;
Maybe it was not wise.
The stones were overturned.
Most of them were broken.
I could not read
The people's names.
The grass was luscious and green,
The flowers were growing wild,
And the hanging branches of the willow tree
Completely bent over.
It was so quiet I could hear the leaves
Moving back and forth.
Under the light breeze, the cows and goats
Were grazing among the graves.
What a shame and disgrace.
I started to cry,
And tears streamed down my face.
I thought,
At least they are at peace.
The six million don't have graves.
Their flesh and bones were burned to ashes
And there is no one to say Kaddish for them.
Just think—six million. It is so easy to say.
Put a face on each number.
With your own eyes and ears,
You won't believe what you have done.
It will haunt you all your life.
So, men and women, bend your knees
Before the Almighty and pray and pray
With all your heart for forgiveness.

The Kaddish

Blessed be the memory forever.
The fields, meadows, forest, valleys are all soaked with your blood.
Your bones are scattered over all the earth;
The soil is fertilized with your ashes,
And the grass grows luscious, tall, and green.
Quickly springing to life, the poppies with red tops
Are bending under the light breeze as if praying for your lost lives.
You have left behind such good, sweet memories.
We, who survived the awful Holocaust,
Remember how you begged for mercy for the children.
Scarcely a soul heard your pleas to save the innocent.
Such a terrible waste it was:
You were all killed because of your race.
Many times in despair—asking, "Where is G-d?"—
You lost your faith, saying, "We haven't done anything wrong."
We believed in Your commandments and tried to live honest lives,
But we didn't stop praying until our last breath.
You called G-d's name and said "Shma Yisroel."
How horribly shameful, heartless and unjust,
To slaughter and gas G-d's people.
Let us work and pray so that tragedies like this
Will never happen again.
We survivors have lost our loved ones,
Those who abide daily in our dreams, hearts, and souls.
When the sky is blue and the sun shines bright, and
When it's dark and cold, our story has to be told.
We will pray for you; we will say Kaddish loud and clear.
We survivors will remind the world that we are still here.

Maria Szapszewicz

WE SURVIVORS

We survivors of the ghettoes and camps,
We suffered, we struggled, we cried and we died.
We tried very hard to lean on each other.
How I always looked out for my mother!
In those bitter, tragic times, she was my only inspiration.
With all my strength, I tried to stay alive,
Not to show my horrid desperation.
I denied my suffering and starvation;
So much time I passed looking through the windows,
Witnessing the heavy smoke mixed with fire
Forming clouds and blotting out the blue sky.
The wind so often played with the fire,
Seeming to blow it my way, taunting me.
Ah, how I wished I could go somewhere,
Someplace where this would be but a bad dream.
But this was my sad reality.
We lived with these horrible pictures every day;
There was not even a spark of hope.
How we wished to make our escape!
But we were fenced in like wild animals in cages.
We looked so horrible—it was so hard to tell our ages.

Most of us looked the same.
We had no names, just numbers on our arms.
Our ashes fertilized the German farms.
Our hair was shorn; we were so lean, so thin;
Our skin was shriveled and yellow.
We were an innocent people.
Our spirits were so low, our hearts so full of fear and pain.

We were condemned to die. We wondered, Why?
What had we done to deserve such a brutal and undeserved end?
Where were the people of the world?
Why would they not stand for us?
This is the inexcusable horror that happened
To the Jews of the twentieth century.

Maria Szapszewicz

FOLLOWING STEPS:
A POEM FOR MY FATHER

I remember you took me to my French lesson,
And I said to you, "Dad, you walk too fast.
I can't follow your steps."
You said to me, "Dear child, walking fast or slow
Is not important to me now."
You slowed down.
You took my hand and gave me a huge hug.
And we walked together.

I remember you, my dearest Father.
You had such a bright smile
When we flew our kites so very high.
You were the one who introduced me to reading books
And said to me, "Don't worry about your looks."

You were young when the Germans killed you
Just because you were a Jew.
They killed your body,
But your spirit still came through.
There were not many Fathers such as you.
You were my stronghold, my fortress,
My hope and inspiration.
You are engraved in my heart and soul
With love and devotion.
I know you dwell now in Paradise,
Where souls are good and righteous.
There is no discrimination.
All live together
Forming one big nation.
I love you, Dad.
I want to tell you, my dear Father, that I still try hard
To follow in your steps.

A Belated Letter to My Mother

I was very lucky being your daughter.
The love and devotion you showed me
Was my greatest treasure,
One that cannot be measured.

We were together during the worst time of our lives,
And I miss you now so much that words cannot express.
My heart alone can tell its sadness and distress.

I was so fortunate to have you for my mother,
Since, as a young girl, I grew up without a father.
I was deprived of basic things in those horrible camps,
And this burned an everlasting stamp.

You were my stronghold, my hope, my inspiration.
I was too shy to show you my great love and devotion.
Without you, I wouldn't have endured to liberation.
You were the one who gave me strength and courage.
You, my dear Mother, gave me
Will and desire to go on and live.

I will always remember you with my greatest love and admiration

Your loving daughter,
Madzia

Don't Cry When I Will Die

(To my dearest children Rose and Joanne)

Don't cry when I will die.
Babies are born,
And old people have to die.

I never believed I would survive the concentration camps.
What the Germans did to us was the one of the worst crimes in
the history
of the world.
What a terrible tragedy this was.
It left me with a broken heart, bruised soul, and broken body.
But there was no choice;
I had to go on living.
Life is so precious and so wonderful,
And nobody has the right to take it away from you.
G-d gave us this most valuable gift: to live.
So don't cry for me.
I tried really hard to live right
And tried not to show you my sorrow.

People are coming,
People are going,
So don't cry.
I believe in a better tomorrow,
And I will be at peace at last.
Where I will be there is no pain.
I will not suffer.
I will hear beautiful music:
Birds singing love songs to each other.
And one day, we will all become one.

All people will be equal, sisters and brothers.
Others will come into the world to build a new life on our ashes,
So don't cry. Just make a better world,
One in which people will live in dignity and peace
And where people will not hurt you because you
Are a Jew, an African American, or someone else
different from them.

> All my love,
> Your Dearest Mother

Maria Szapszewicz

THE LAST REMNANTS

We survivors of the Holocaust are dying one by one.
Each day there are fewer of us left.

Now the time moves on so very fast and escapes us.
We who carry the heavy burden of those terrible memories,
We try to tell our stories of wounds that never were healed.
We open wounds which were only partially sealed.

We want to tell the people of the world
What happened to our Mothers, Children, Fathers,
Whole families killed.
Our hearts and souls are with those left behind.

While we live, they live in our memories.
It's so hard to deal with, and nobody understands.
Only those who went through the long sleepless nights
Understand the nightmares on the rare nights we are able to sleep.

Oh, those terrible dreams. Waking up
In the middle of the night, soaked with sweat,
Full of confusion, even when you know where you are.
As you try to escape them, they follow you
And stay with you forever.

It is such a horrible sadness.
We will never understand
The Germans' madness.

Jacob's great-great-grandfather in Smylow, Poland. Farmland had been given to him and his family in the nineteenth century for saving a Polish general's life.

Maria's boyfriend Jakob Kirschenbaum, who
died of tuberculosis in Czechoslovakia after
the war.

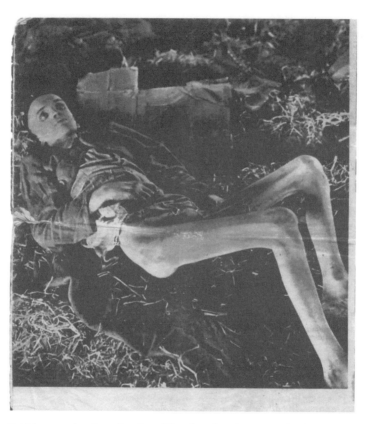

British paper showing what the soldiers found in the camps after liberating it.

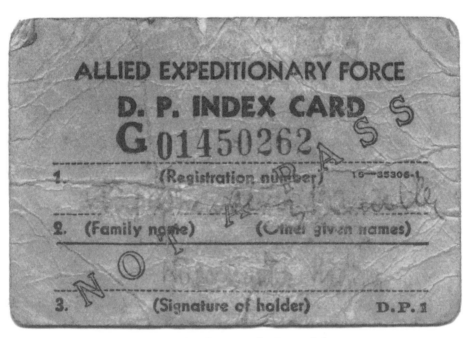

Maria's DP Identification card at Bergen-Belsen.

AUSSCHUSS
EHEMALIGER KONZENTRATIONS-HÄFTLINGE

HANNOVER
FRIEDRICHSTR. 8a

Dr.K./Km.   den 29 ... .

Frl. Weizhändler, Marie   28.2.192...
....
ist ein ehemaliger Konzentrationslager-Häftling.
will seine Familie ... sich ebenfalls im Konzen-
trationsla ... ... befinde. Falls die en...
lische Be ... ... eine solche Reise ... ...
wenden hab ... ... wandersrecht bei ... ...
... .

Frl. Weizhändler, Marie
....

Wir bitten, ...   auf ...
behilflich su ... .

s. Weizhändler, Marie   28.2.192...
....
is a former concentration - risoner. He ... to
search his fa ... which also are in concentr ...
camps. If the ... lish Authorities have no ...
against this journey, we, I on our part ha ...
hesitation.

We ask for ... ... of his
.x/p.

Weizhändler, Marie
....

Affidavit/Certificate confirming that Maria was indeed who she claimed.

Hermann Goerring's headquarters were used as a DP camp at Bergen-Belsen after the war; here are Maria's aunt, her brother Henry, and her aunt's husband and child.

Maria at the DP camp in
Bergen-Belsen, c. 1947.

Maria working with committee members in the DP camp at Bergen=Belsen at the end of 1945; brother Henry (l) and and Miss Friedmann (r).

The first Seder service at Bergen-Belsen DP Camp.

Maria's brother Henry, Pearl Wajchendler and her husband, a Romanian friend, and Maria.

1947, another wedding at the Bergen-Belsen DP Camp.

Maria, second from right, a friend of the bride, at her wedding in the Bergen-Belsen DP Camp.

Maria stopped in Poland during a trip to see a sick friend in Czechoslovakia in 1947. Maria (lower left), sister-in-law Tosia (upper right)

Maria (third from end, left row) demonstrating over the British refusal to allow passengers of the *Exodus* to disembark in Palestine, July 1947.

Maria's good friend Helen on the first Aliyah Bet transport from Bergen-Belsen DP camp to Israel.

Maria helps refugees at Bergen-Belsen DP camp with their food and housing needs.
She also was in charge of the employment office.

Sara Wajchendler and her children, Henry and Maria.

Hermann Goerring's former officers camp becomes a DP camp; Maria's brother Henry and his girl friend playing tennis.

Dr. Tosia Szapszewicz, Jacob's sister, visiting Zbyszek, Jacob's best childhood-friend. A member of the Armja Krajowa, an anti-Semitic and anti-German partisan unit, Zbyszek nonetheless saved Jacob from being killed by his fellow partisans.

Maria's mother and brother in Switzerland.

Daughter Rose, 1951, in Lodz, Poland.

Daughter Rose at the Baltic Sea, 1955.

Jacob, surrounded by daughters Rose (l.) and Joanne (r.) shortly before
leaving Lodz, Poland for the U.S.

Jacob and his sister, Dr. Tosia Szapszewwicz, at a fountain in the resort at Ciechocinek, 1958.

Jacob with daughter Joanne in the U.S.

Maria's mother, Sara Wajchendler, in Forest Park,
St. Louis, Missouri.

Jacob and his sister Tosia's husband, George Henkel, 1958.

Picture of Maria in Communist Poland, c. late-1950's.

Jacob in St. Louis, 1970.

Maria, surrounded by daughters Rose (l.) and Joanne (r.) in Forest Park, St. Louis, Missouri.

Jacob Szapszewicz, Maria's husband.

Jacob's graduation with his M.B.A. from Washington University in St. Louis, 1964.

Joanne Szapszewicz and Suzanne Goodmann and at their
high school graduation, c. 1978.

Jacob and granddaughter Marise at Senior Olympics, May 1989.

Jacob sitting on a couch at daughter Joanne's, c. 1997.

Missouri Govenor Mel Carnahan, Maria, and her grandchildren Marisa and Ariella, May 1998.

Maria with students from All Saints Academy (Breese, IL) following her presentation at the Holocaust Museum and Learning Center in St. Louis.

Maria Szapszewicz

Essays, Stories

AND AN

Interview

ON THE

Holocaust

THE FINAL SELECTION IN LABOR CAMP

I remember it vividly, as if it happened today. It was the beginning of spring, but the weather was still cold and windy. At least, after the long winter, the sun would shine, providing warmth to our bodies, and the sky would be blue. The days would be longer, we would not have to work to work in the dark, and we would have a little more daylight in the barrack. Springtime always brought a little hope, but we all were very discouraged. It was the third year of the war, and there had been no change for the better. It was hard to go on. Suffering as we were from intense hunger and all manner of diseases, we were fenced in and watched closely by guards. It was impossible to wash ourselves with the freezing cold water, and even going to the outside toilet in the cold was a tremendous effort. We thought only of food and our loved ones.

We forced ourselves to work with our last ounce of strength, but there came a time when we could do nothing more, because most of us were quite sick. A terrible epidemic of typhoid had broken out. Most of the victims simply lay on their bunk beds and begged for water, but there was no one to give them food or drink. Any who were able to work were in the munitions factory, so there was no one to tend to the ill. One by one, the sick people died, often crying out for their mothers in their semi-conscious, delirious state.

My mother was infected with typhoid and was very ill. I was very worried and in despair. I had to leave her each day and go to work, but I always left a container of water near her, and, when I returned each day, I washed her burning face with cold water and tried to feed her some soup. All my efforts were poured into caring for her. In the camp, there were no doctors, since they had to work in the munitions factory like everyone else. There were no medications available, so we either got better on or own or died.

The Germans were furious that so many people were sick and unable to work for them. They decided to get rid of the sick and the weak. Since it did not pay for them to transport the victims to an extermination camp to be gassed and burned, they called in a special Einsatzgruppen battalion. Who developed a special method for determining who was fit to work. They gathered up some people, handed them shovels, and forced them to dig a ditch and fill it with water. Then they killed the people who had dug the trench. Later, guards burst into the barrack, beating us and crying, "Out, out, you dirty Jews!" Those who were unable to move were shot in their bunk beds; the rest were beaten and forced to run and jump over the ditch filled with water. Some fell in to the dirty ditch, and others tried to help them. It was a terrible scene, so hard to force myself to describe, yet I know I must. Those who fell into the ditch were eventually gathered up and placed in trucks to be hauled away for execution.

All this time, I was beside myself, not knowing what to do about my mother. Without even thinking, I put her into a straw sack and covered her with another straw sack. I then started to run down the hill and over the ditch. The Einsatzgruppen were yelling at us to form a ring, and behind them were other Germans with guns pointed at us. In the middle were some members of the Gestapo S.S., high-ranking officials. I looked around and realized that my brother was on a transport truck with the sick, doomed to death. In just a second, I began to run toward the center of the ring, where I spotted the officer who was in charge of the selection. The Germans raised their guns to kill me, but the officer called out to them, "Wait! Don't shoot!" I was standing before him and started to recite a beautiful German poem. I had studied German in school before the war, and this was my favorite poem. He looked at me, puzzled, and asked, "Are you German?" I replied, "No. I am a Jew."

"What do you want?" he asked. I said, "I want you to save my brother. He is in the transport truck with the sick who are going to be killed." For a split second, I had touched his heart. He said, "I will spare him," but then he was ashamed that he had had some human feelings and declared, "All the Jews will be killed, so it doesn't matter if it is sooner or later." He got into his car and signaled to the other Germans to move on.

I ran quickly to the truck where my brother was being held and told the guard that the officer said to remove my brother. They looked at me but took my brother down. The trucks with the sick then drove in to the woods, where the passengers were killed.

That is how I saved my dear brother Henry, but I still did not know the fate of my mother. I was worried that she may have suffocated. I ran back to the barrack and saw that the guards had cut the straw sacks with bayonets to be sure no one was hidden inside. My heart stopped beating. I gathered all my courage and pulled off the sack in which she was hiding. She opened her beautiful blue eyes and asked, "What is going on?" I started to cry from joy and happiness. I was unable to speak but simply kept crying and crying.

After the selection, the elderly block leader came up to me and asked, "What did you say to the German officer that made him save your brother and your mother?" I never revealed the truth, though, because I knew the block leaders collaborated with the Germans, and I was afraid harm to my family would result.

My younger brother was killed in Mauthausen, and my father died in the Lodz Ghetto. Thanks to G-d, my brother, my mother, and I all survived the war. We rebuilt our lives, and my brother and I married and had children. Here I record our story so the world will know what the Germans did.

THE PRECIOUS COAT

During the war, I worked in an ammunition factory called Hermann Goering Werke. Before the war, the town in which the factory was located was a shtetl where about five thousand Jews lived. Shortly before the war broke out, the Poles changed the name of the shtetl from Wierzbnik to Starachowice, and on the outskirts of the town they built huge ammunition factories.

These factories brought to the town new people and great prosperity. When the war broke out, in no time the Germans overpowered Poland and occupied the town. They took over the ammunition factories, changed the administration, let many people go and replaced them with Jews, who worked as slave laborers. They forced us into camp and watched over us with S.S. guards and Ukrainians.

Every worker in the camp was assigned to a very narrow space in the barracks, which were arranged with bunks. They were so narrow that one could hardly move. Every body was given a straw sack but no blankets whatsoever. On those bunk beds, we lived and slept. We tried to cover ourselves with whatever we could. I was very lucky in that I had a coat. My neighbor on the bunk had nothing, so we shared the coat and covered ourselves with it,. The coat was not large enough to cover our bodies; it covered the top portions of our bodies, but our feet would stick out. The nights were so cold that we would wake up freezing. To be honest, we each began pulling on the coat as we slept until finally it tore in two. I as in despair and started to cry. I was very angry, because now I couldn't even wear the coat anymore to work.

At the factory, we worked with Christians. They were free people and lived in their own homes. How I envied them! As the guards marched us to the factories with big dogs, I was sleepy, hungry, thirsty and cold. I could see the homes of the Christians as we passed by, with bright lights and smoke coming out of the chimneys. I knew they were cooking breakfast, and I could smell the hot coffee. It drove me nearly mad. Here I was locked up, and I didn't even have my coat that meant so much to me. It was my most precious possession; it had sheltered me from the freezing weather during the night and day. I had no choice but to start to work without it. I was very sad, and my eyes were swollen from crying.

Suddenly, almost from out of nowhere, a man walked up to me and asked what had happened. He could tell from looking at me how upset I was, even under already trying circumstances. I was afraid of him, but he said, "Don't be frightened. I want to help you." I did not trust him, because I had been disappointed too many times already. But somehow, in spite of everything, I told him what had happened with the coat. He replied, "My dear child, don't worry. Next morning, I will bring you some thread and a needle."

I didn't believe him, but the next day when I came to work there was a small package on the machine which I operated. I was afraid to touch it, because many times the Germans pulled tricks on us and accused us of stealing so they could punish us. As I was pondering this, to my surprise the man from yesterday came up to me and said, "Open the package. What is the matter with you?" When I did so, I found a needle, thread, a slice of bread and a hard-boiled egg. He said, "Why don't' you eat?" I answered that I wanted to share the egg with my mother, since she was even hungrier than I. "Don't worry, he assured me. Tomorrow I will bring something for your mother."

So, my dears, there were some good people in those awful times. Perhaps not too many, but every person who had the courage to stand up for justice was a great hero to me, and I salute them. May G-d bless them!

The Schwartze Laja

My dear husband Jacob, who was born in the village of Smylow, told this story.

A large and devoted family with three sisters and four brothers, and the only Jewish family in the village, they owned a very large farm with a huge lake and a flour mill with a water mill. How Jacob loved to watch the water splashing on the wheel and forming crystals. How he liked to swim in the lake and take a boat out to catch fish. They also owned some horses, carriages, cows, chickens, geese, and ducklings. Their mother had hired help to take care of the household and oversaw everything. She liked to milk the cows and made cheese from the milk, and they kept a strictly kosher household.

This farm was located in a shtetl called Szydlowiec, where about six thousand Jews lived. They were mostly very poor in money but rich in spirit, and they strictly observed the religion. This shtetl had a rabbi, who was head of the Jewish community and who kept in constant contact with the police and mayor of the city. The rabbi handled marriages, divorces, and births and settled all kinds of disputes. His position resembled that of a judge, and people had to observe his judgments. He was able to live comfortably; his house contained a special office and a waiting room, which was always full of the many people needing to see him. The officials, however (such as the police and firefighters), did not have to wait. The rebbetzin and the two daughters took care of the house and kept a kosher diet. They always bought food from trustworthy people so they could trust that everything was kosher. They knew for certain that the cheese my mother-in-law made was kosher. She sold it for a small price to a poor widow who had many children so that that widow could make a living.

This Schwartze Laja sold cheese to the rebbetzin, and one fine day she came to the village to get some of the cheese. It was a hot day, she had just walked several miles, and she had grown very tired. When she arrived, my mother-in-law told her to rest and gave her something to drink and eat. She was in a terrible rush, though; she wanted to get to the rabbi's house before sundown. She took the cheese and loaded it into her basket, covering each of the cheeses with horseradish, since she had no paper, which was expensive back then.

With the hot sun shining brightly overhead, she started to walk back to the shtetl on this beautiful, cloudless day. Laja was so tired from carrying such a heavy load that she decided to take a short cut through the fields. It was harvest time, and the wheat was already cut and arranged neatly in bundles and columns. She decided to take a short break, but all of a sudden she had a terrible stomachache. She felt like relieving her bowels, but she was in a field, and there weren't any bathrooms. So she pushed aside the wheat and relieved herself both ways—she pooped and peed—in the stacks. Then she noticed to her delight that there were several packages of printed paper. Overjoyed and in near-disbelief, she said, "Oh G-d, thank you for this paper!" The heavens had opened and shone down upon her. People hadn't liked their cheese wrapped in horseradish, and now she could wrap the cheeses in paper!

She went into town, where her first stop was the rabbi. After the rebbezin bought the cheeses needed, she set out to sell what was left. Laja was so happy, she forgot she was tired. She thought, "My G-d! Rizelah almost gave me the cheese for nothing. Now she can get some money for her efforts; now she will help the poor people. Laja asked G-d to bless Rizelah with good health. Laja waited in the waiting room, which was full of people. All of a sudden, she heard a noise. Someone said that the chief of police was coming and that everyone should make room to let him through. He looked around and noticed that Laja had a great deal of paper. Though unable to read Polish, she held the paper, and he began to shout, "You are a communist! You came here to give out paper to people!" She started to cry and tearfully asked, "Me, a communist? What's a communist?'" The policeman started to say, "Don't play stupid games with me, Laja. You're not as innocent as you look."

The rabbi heard the noise and tried to get out. In the meantime, he said, "What's going on here?" Laja, with cuffs on her hands, just continued to cry. Speaking in Yiddish, the rabbi said, "What have you done, Laja?" She answered, "I don't know," and continued to cry. The rabbi said, "My G-d! Where the hell did you get all that paper?" She said, "I found it when I went out to relieve myself and took it because I needed paper for the cheeses I sell." The rabbi addressed the chief of police, "Let me explain. She is definitely no communist. She just can't read Polish." The policeman asked where she had gotten the papers, and the rabbi looked at her and asked, "Laja, where did you get the paper?" Laja was ashamed because she made a **kupa** (bowel movement) and explained that she had gotten them from a stack of wheat and that there were still more. They put Laja into a cart and drove her to the field, where they found the rest of the papers, and they took away the paper she had. The rabbi made it clear that she was innocent and that she just couldn't read.

Laja went home to her children and told them the story of what had happened to her. The Schwartze Laja perished with her children in the Holocaust. I am telling this story because the Jews were very poor, but this story will be here for many more generations, and everyone will know that there was once a shtetl where Jews lived in harmony and that there was once this vibrant community which no longer exists. May the memory of all those who died in the war be blessed to all of us.

The Altar Boy

Jacob was born in Smylow, which was a good-sized village where about thirty or forty families lived. Most of these were peasants who owned small parcels of land where they grew potatoes, which was their main food source. They were poor people. Some had a little business, such as a grocery story, a hardware store, or a butcher shop. They had many children, and these ran around without supervision. Some of them went to school, but some had to help their parents on the farms and never received an education.

The Szapszewicz family was the only Jewish family that lived in this village. They had a very large farm with orchards, fields, and a large lake with all kinds of fish in it. They also had a water-powered flour mill with a huge wheel, and they served the community by grinding all the flour in the area. The peasants wondered why this Jewish family wanted to live among the Christians. Why didn't they live in their own community in the shtetl where all the Jews lived? They didn't know that a Polish prince had given them this land centuries ago. The Helfands (Jacob's mother's family) had helped this prince when the Germans occupied Poland by hiding him safely. The peasants respected the family because the Szapszewicz family helped them in every possible way, and the family was on good terns with the community. The children played together, except on the Jewish Sabbath and holidays, when the father went to the Jewish shtetl with the boys to pray in the synagogue.

On Sunday, the Christians went to church all dressed in their Sunday best. They always walked barefoot until they were a few yards away from the church. Then, in order to preserve them as long as possible, they put on their shoes. On Sundays, with his friends at church, Jacob was very lonely. He started to follow them and waited for them outside of the church until the services were over, no matter how bad the weather was outside. Longing to play with the others, he hid under a tree when it rained or snowed, no matter how windy it was.

One Sunday, the priest spied him as he walked to the rectory to get something he had forgotten. The priest asked Jacob what he was doing there under the tree during the services. Jacob told him he was waiting for the boys with whom he would be playing soccer later. This particular Sunday was especially cold, and the priest beckoned him to come into the church. Jacob hesitated at first because it was unheard of for an observant Jew to enter a Catholic church. Inside, he was very surprised and impressed to see his best buddy dressed in a long, white robe and carrying a large cross. After the Mass, the priest came up to Jacob and asked him if he liked their service and if he knew how to read Latin. Jacob told him he could both read write in Latin, and he liked to read all the time. Then, the priest asked him if he would like to be an altar boy. Jacob was delighted and very flattered and responded that he would love to be an altar boy. The priest tested him and told him, "You have a good head. You will be my altar boy. Those other boys can't remember anything." Jacob learned the prayers and rituals very quickly.

The peasants wondered why a Jewish boy had become an altar boy. One Sunday after the Catholic services, some of the peasants stopped by the Szapszewicz home and asked Jacob's father why a Jewish boy was an altar boy at the Catholic church. What was he doing there? This was surprising news to Bernard, and he answered that it must be someone else. One of the peasants assured Bernard that it was indeed "Jake"; he and his own son were always together.

Bernard decided to go to the church to find out what was going on. When Jacob was leaving the church after the Mass, Bernard grabbed him by the ear and dragged him home, with Jacob screaming in pain. Bernard was furious that his son had lied to him, telling him he was playing soccer with the other boys, while in fact he had become an altar boy at the church. Bernard was very strict with his children, and Jacob knew he was in very big trouble. When they reached home, Bernard took off his belt, and Jacob received a bare-butt spanking, after which he couldn't sit down for several days. He never forgot the beating he had received for lying to his father about being an altar boy. It was a powerful lesson on the importance of honesty for the rest of his life.

The Roosters Are Crowing

My beloved husband Jacob Szapszewicz told this story. It is a true story.

It was a very cold winter's night, and the wind was blowing strongly. The snow was falling, and it covered the earth like a white blanket. Jacob and his family lived in a village where they had a beautiful, large farm with a large lake, orchards, fields covered with wheat, and a waterfall flour-mill. Jacob liked to watch the mill's big wheel turn and splash water like a mist which reflected the colors of the rainbow. Jacob's family had been privileged to own the farm for many years and were the envy of the whole village since the peasants owned just small parcels of land on which they mostly grew potatoes. Because Jacob's family was Jewish, the peasants did not like them, but the peasants tolerated Jacob's family because they always needed something from them.

Since Jacob's family lived very primitively and had neither running water nor electricity, someone had to fill a huge barrel sitting in the kitchen with water brought from the well outside. When it got dark, the family used candles or an oil lamp to see. They slept under huge down comforters, which kept them very warm. When the family woke up, these comforters were covered with ice crystals which formed from their breath during the night. Although there was no heat at night, they lived a happy and healthy life. They ate fresh food which they had grown themselves, and they were content with their life.

There was no school in the village, but there was a public school (which only went to the sixth grade) which Jacob and his siblings attended in the shetl. In addition, Jacob's father hired a malamed (a rabbi) who came to the house and taught them religious studies. When Jacob graduated from the public school, he wanted to continue his education, but his parents were not happy because the upper school was in another town, and Jacob would need to take a train to get there. The village was located about five miles from the train station, and Jacob would need to walk that distance through the forest to reach the train. But Jacob wanted to study so badly that he promised his parents he would get up early and walk to the train no matter what kind of weather it was, even when it was as harsh and icy as it was that night.

His mother was always up early to start the morning fire in the stove, and, after the kitchen was warmed up, she woke up Jake. The night was exceptionally cold, and there were snow flurries outside. In the morning, the windows were covered with frost resembling blossoming flowers. Although they didn't have a hanging clock, and although Jacob's father owned a pocket watch of which he was very proud and wouldn't let anyone touch, they simply estimated the time in the morning by the crowing of the roosters since they didn't want to wake up Bernard (Jacob's father). They always went to bed early in the winter, but first they told stories by the oil lamp or the candles. And some of the peasants came to hear these stories.

Jacob always had homework to do or books to read. After finishing his homework, Jacob went to bed, but he immediately heard his mother cry out, "Get up! Get up! Hurry up. It's late!" He stretched his body, got out of bed, put on warm woolen socks, and washed his face. She continued to hurry him up because she thought he would be late for the train which stopped at the station a few miles from the village. Jacob had to walk through the woods in the dark. Having a vivid imagination and a great fear that wolves would chase him, he started to run and fell. When he finally reached the train terminal, he was certain he had missed the train since no one else was there; usually, there were peasants, merchants, and business people taking their goods to town. Although it was quiet, Jacob was afraid to return home, and he started to cry. Then he looked up and saw the conductor at the station. He asked Jacob was he was doing there at midnight. Jacob explained that his mother had awakened him and told him he would be late if he didn't hurry. Jacob had barely been able to keep his eyes open. Because Jacob had helped him many times, the conductor liked him and told him to lie down on the wooden bench and go back to sleep. He covered him up with his longhaired shepherd's coat and told Jacob he would wake him up when it was time to go.

When he returned from school that afternoon, he asked his mother why she had awakened him so early. She explained that she had done so because the roosters were crowing and she thought it was time for Jacob to get up and go to school. Unfortunately, that night, the roosters had simply made a mistake.

THE EGGS

I used to love to listen to Jacob's stories. This one is his egg story.

A farm is a wonderful place to raise children, and, although Jews seldom lived on farms, Jacob's family had owned their beautiful farm for centuries. It had a large lake filled with fish, and children waded or fished in it in the summer. They were splashing each other and having fun. In the winter, when the lake was frozen, the boys and the braver girls skated with homemade wooden skates because they couldn't afford to buy skates. Often, the ice would break, and the children fell into the water and screamed for help. The really smart ones, however, skated on the edge of the lake. The farm had a large barn with cows, horses, and a chicken coop. There were orchards with all kinds of fruit, such as apples, plums, pears, and cherries. And there was a flour mill with an enormous wooden water wheel.

Every morning, Jacob went out with a basket to gather the fresh-laid eggs from the chicken coop. Some chickens were proud of having laid their eggs. They clucked about it and shook their feathers with pride. Jacob had to be especially sneaky to get the eggs from them.

On the way home from the barn, Jacob liked to sample some of the raw eggs, but he didn't want anyone to know what he had done. He thought and thought, and he came up with a way to suck the inside of the egg out of the shell without hurting it; he punched two very small holes in the egg with a nail from his pocket, in which he kept all kinds of things. This way, no one would suspect that the egg was empty. When he brought the basket home and his mother inspected them, she wondered if some chickens had laid empty eggs. He laughed and then explained that these weren't miracle eggs. He had simply extracted the yolk and the whites by sucking them out. (He and his mother were very close. He was her favorite son and seemed unable to do any wrong in her eyes. She told him stories, and he listened to her.)

The years passed, and Jake grew up. He served in the military, went to college, and got a job. That was when the war broke out and the Germans conquered Poland. It was a very hard time, and food was scarce. The Germans put Jews in ghettos and made some of the young people work in slave labor camps. They killed young and old.

Early one morning, the shtetl was surrounded by Germans who took the Jews to the train station and put them in cattle cars. The Germans were pushing, yelling, and beating people with rods, and everybody was very confused. Children were crying, looking for their parents, and the young and healthy were put on trucks and taken to a nearby town where there was a huge munitions factory where they were put to work. They lived in a fence-in camp guarded by Germans with machine guns, and they slept in crowded barracks on bunks without blankets or pillows. Water and toilet facilities were outside. They received very meager food, a starvation diet consisting of a slice of bread, thin soup, and some kind of warm liquid.

In this setting, Jacob remembered how good it had been before the war when he had lived on the farm. Working in the factory now was very hard. No one had good clothes for the winter, and it was very cold. People couldn't wash themselves properly, and a terrible epidemic of typhus, as well as of other diseases, broke out. In a way, Jacob was lucky. He didn't become sick, because he had already recovered from typhus earlier.

When he and the other factory workers returned to the camp, he heard someone yell, "You sons of bitches. Do we have a surprise for you." The block leaders, carrying baskets filled with eggs, shouted, "Line up. Every one of you men is going to get two eggs." The girls, however, got nothing. The men were astounded. What was going on? First, they ate their bread, and they saved the eggs for later. In just a few minutes, though, they heard a voice over the loudspeaker order, "Don't eat those eggs. Anyone who does will be severely punished." The workers immediately saw the block leaders running with empty baskets and shouting, "Out, out, and bring the eggs with you. Put them back into the baskets now!" When Jacob heard this, he took a hatpin out of his cap and carefully pierced the eggs, remembering how he had sucked the inside of the eggs out when he was a young boy on the farm. He did this very carefully, leaving the eggs intact but very empty. Then, walking proudly and confidently, he placed his perfect-looking eggs back into the German's basket. It appeared that the block leaders had made a mistake; they were supposed to give the eggs to the German guards and workers, not to the Jewish inmates, and these block leaders were punished. Jacob strolled innocently back to his bunk with a full stomach and a smile on his face.

SIMON WHO FOUGHT BACK

Dear Simon, I will always remember you. You were so young, so full of energy, and had such a zest for life. You had such a good heart and tried to help everybody. This story was told to us by a peasant who was present and was assigned the task of burying you.

It happened that your brother was badly injured in the slave labor camp by the guards. The Germans had organized a ghetto for the weak and sick and for those who were in hiding with false identification papers. The Germans had given assurance that all these people could come to the ghetto and would be able to live in safe conditions. Your brother was sent to this ghetto, and you followed him. At the time, you were working and had a chance to survive, but you chose to go be with him.

The Germans had lied, however, and they sent all these people to Auschwitz, where they were gassed and burned. You had so much courage. You took a great risk and somehow escaped from the selection, perhaps by jumping over a fence when the guard wasn't looking or by crawling through a hole underneath. You made it back to your family farm and met a childhood friend, a Christian. He was surprised to see you. He offered you help and shelter. But you did not trust him, and you were right. Townspeople in the village informed you that he belonged to an underground anti-Semitic organization that hunted down Jews and killed them. They would receive a kilo of sugar from the Germans for turning in a Jew-this was the price of a Jewish life.

Not knowing what to do in the village, you decided to return to the labor camp and rejoin the working Jews who worked for an ammunition factory. The guard noticed a new Jew among the ranks, however, and took you away to the camp jail, where you were beaten and deprived of food. You were so brave; you did not give up. You broke the bars from the windows and tried to escape. But bad luck followed you. The guards caught you and returned you to the cell, this time in chains. The next day, they took you to the woods and forced you to dig your own grave. The guards gave you a shovel and made fun of you as you dug, calling you all sorts of names. You did not give up, in spite of everything. In a split second, you saw your chance. You turned and struck the guard next to you with the shovel. You injured him, but, before you could do more, two other guards instantly struck you and injured you.

Dear Simon, you were only eighteen years old. The family who survived the Holocaust will always remember your courage and your will to live. You are inscribed in our hearts with love.

THE COURAGEOUS RIVKA

The shtetl of Szydlowiec was not too far from the large city of Radom. In this shtetl there lived about 6,000 Jews and a small percentage of Christians. The Christians mostly lived on the outskirts of the shtetl. This shtetl had existed for centuries and contained an old castle which was surrounded by water.

The Jews who lived in there had all types of professions. Some were tailors. There were a few families who owned small factories for leather work. There were also button factories and small grocery shops. The young girls who worked in the button factory sewed buttons onto cards. They worked extremely long hours and were paid close to nothing. It was indeed very hard for most of the people to make a living. However, they tried to live in the present and not to worry too much about the future. In addition, they were careful to try to save a portion of their earnings for a festive Shabbat. Most of the inhabitants of the shtetl were very religious and studied torah all day long.

The women had many children—there were many new pregnancies each year—and it was the women's responsibility to provide everything for the household. My husband's family, the only Jewish family in the village, had a large farm near that particular shtetl. My husband, Jacob, told me this story. I loved to listen to his stories for he is a phenomenal storyteller.

Growing up, I lived in a big city, and my father had a prominent business. During the winter, these Jews especially felt their poverty, and bitter cold penetrated their skin. The snow covered the earth like a soft blanket. Rivka, a woman who lived in the shtetl, stayed home with the children and her husband on the cold evenings. They had no heat, and the children needed warmth and nourishment. They cried in their misery and tried to warm each other with the heat from their bodies. Unfortunately, Rivka did not have any food. Though hungry and in despair, she was a very strong-willed woman with a lot of energy. She put this energy to good use by getting out of her bed. She dressed up with a skirt and her husband's boots and had the good idea of stuffing paper into them in order to make them fit properly. Then Rivka tried to get out of her house. She shoveled away the snow when she realized that this day was market day, and she prayed G-d to help her feed her children.

She walked around and spotted a peasant standing on the road. She stopped him and asked, "What do you have? I can smell a strong odor." He replied, "I have some fish in the bathtub." She said, "Listen. Would you like me to sell those fish for you since it is nearly Shabbat?"

She strolled down to the fish market, and the peasant, who was cold from traveling such a long distance, asked her for directions to an inn so he could warm up. He told her he'd leave the fish to her because he trusted her. Rivka was delighted and thought, G-d is good to me. However, not many customers wanted to purchase food in the cold, and her hands became very cold and numb. People in the market usually warmed their hands over a pot of burning wood and coal. She moved towards the warmth and cried out for customers. All of a sudden, people frantically shouted, "Rivka is on fire!" for she had accidentally turned over the pot. Everyone stared at her in awe but did absolutely nothing at all to aid her. All of a sudden, Jacob, who had been visiting friends in town, heard all of the commotion and sprinted towards Rivka. He lifted her with his strong hands and threw her into the fish-filled bathtub. She was indeed grateful for that, though, by the end of the night, she was still empty-handed and soaking wet.

Jacob took her home to her children and husband. She sobbed because she had not managed to bring food or money to her family. Jacob said, "Don't cry. I will be back soon." Jacob proceeded to a bakery and bought some food for Rivka and her family. Everyone was fed that night, and their hunger problem was at least temporarily solved.

These incidents occurred just before Hitler conquered Poland. Soon, the Nazis would rush in and kill Rivka's whole family. Now, there are no longer any shtetls. That part of Jewish culture and most of the Jewish people who were part of it have sadly perished.

THE MISCHIEVOUS DIAMOND

My mother owned a beautiful diamond engagement ring. I remember it so vividly. Since my earliest childhood, I was always fascinated by it and loved to behold it. It was so radiant that it sparkled like a shining star, blinding my eyes with rays of fire.

This diamond ring had a very interesting story to it. First of all, it had belonged to our family for generations—I should say for a few centuries—and had graced the fingers of many brides. It was always passed to the youngest man in the family as an engagement ring for the future bride. It happened that my father was the youngest of the four sons in his family, and my dear mother was the lucky bride to receive the ring. My mother was very proud and happy to show off such a beautiful piece of jewelry. She wore it with so much pleasure and treasured it as a priceless heirloom.

But heavy clouds were hanging over Europe. Hitler came to power in Germany and invaded Poland on September 1, 1939. In no time at all, he began to place restrictions on the Jewish people. First, it was decreed that the Jews would have to declare all their money and jewelry and turn them over to German officials. Whoever did not obey would be severely punished. My parents gave up a lot of jewelry and valuables, but my mother decided not to turn in the precious diamond she loved so much. She stopped wearing the ring and hid it. At the time, my brothers and I were not even aware of what she had done.

As part of their planned persecution, the Germans soon drove us out of our beautiful apartment and herded us into a ghetto, where we shared a small room with another family. We were very fortunate, however, because my father was appointed to deliver his goods to the Germans. He was a very successful businessman, and he was given special permission to leave the ghetto at appointed times—under the supervision of guards, of course. But many times he was able to bring back some food for us, since the amount of food in the ghetto was very restricted and we were hungry all the time.

Former employees of my father tried to help us. They hated the Germans for what they had done, and they knew we were locked in the ghetto. A former manager, a very righteous Christian, decided to help us out of the ghetto, although he knew my father would have to stay since he was required to work directly for the Germans. He managed to smuggle us out by bribing a guard whom he used to know before the war. We traveled a few days and arrived in the little village where my grandparents used to live. There we shared an apartment with my mother's family. It was very crowded, but we were very happy to be there. Life was harsh, and we were starving.

Once I overheard my uncle ask my mother, "Sara, what did you do with your beautiful ring? Did you turn it over to the Germans?" She informed him that she had not done so, but at this time she was not sure what to do with the ring. Since she had been born and raised in this village—or shtetl, as we called it—she still had some friends from her childhood there and some distant relatives. One of them was a very learned and wise man whom she trusted very much. He truly was a fine man. She decided to tell him about the diamond and ask his advice. Where could she hide the diamond and yet still keep it safe with her? The wise man advised her to place it in the heel of her shoe. However, it first had to be placed there by a competent and trustworthy shoemaker. No problem—the wise man knew of an excellent shoemaker, a very religious man in whom he placed the highest confidence.

My mother visited the shoemaker and told him her story and how the wise man had sent her there. The shoemaker replied that he would be happy to aid her. He drilled a small hole into the heel of the shoe and, after placing the diamond within it, covered it with a few layers of leather. My mother guarded the shoes with her life. She used to say that, even as she fell asleep, she tried to keep one eye on her shoes. We often wondered what she meant!

In time, the Germans sent us from the ghetto to a labor camp, where my mother and I were separated from my brothers. We worked in an ammunitions factory. Each day, we had to march a few miles from the barrack to the factory. Naturally, my mother's shoes began to wear out, especially the heels. They needed to be repaired, and she asked a guard if there was a shoemaker nearby who could help her. He gave her special permission to have the shoes repaired. Since she couldn't walk barefoot, she asked me to take them to the shop and told me to watch the shoemaker because she had a diamond hidden deep in the heel. I opened my eyes wide, scarcely able to believe that she had risked her life in such a fashion.

I took the shoes to the cobbler and asked him if he could repair them while I waited. He asked why such a hurry, and I replied that my mother had to go to work in a few hours. He agreed, and I watched him closely as he worked. When he finished, I returned the shoes to my mother, who asked me if I had watched him carefully. I assured her that I had never taken my eyes off him. She was very happy and said, "Maybe the war will be over before they need to be repaired again." She was wrong. Every day, we had to walk back and forth from the barrack to the factory, always hungry and tired from the hard work. The war seemed to drag on and on.

In the ammunitions factory, we worked alongside some Christians who were free people. Some of them belonged to underground organizations, and they tried to help us. Many times they sympathized with us and gave us bread. A couple of them, two men, seemed particularly kind and gracious. My mother placed great trust in them. She confided to them one day that she had hidden some money and silver back in the cellar of the building where we lived in the ghetto. They told her they would be happy to get the valuables out for her so she could exchange them for bread. She drew a map for them. In the morning, they brought us food and some of the valuables. With the things we had collected, we were able to exchange them for a little food. Even so, we were still always hungry; it was impossible to live on the amount of food we were given. We knew that sooner or later we would die from starvation.

One day my mother told me that she couldn't stand it any longer to watch us starve. She sometimes saw my brothers passing by the factory, and she came up with an idea. She said to me, "I am going to sell my diamond." I was very surprised that she had made such a decision, knowing how precious this diamond was to her and all the memories it held. Then she added, "I would like to keep it, but our lives are more important than memories and sentiments." I asked how she planned to remove it from the heel of her shoe. She told me that she was going to ask the guard to permission for my brother to visit her, and then the two of them would manage to remove the diamond.

We bribed the guard, and he gave my brother a pass to see my mother. We all were very excited and couldn't wait for the moment to see him. The lucky day came, and he arrived. He was aware of what my mother wanted him to do. He brought with him a small pair of pliers. He came up to the bunk bed in our barrack where we stayed, and my mother removed her shoe. My brother knew he needed to hurry because he only had been given permission to visit for half an hour. He pulled with all his might and loosened the heel. We were astonished to discover that the diamond was not inside! My mother was very frustrated and began to cry, blaming me that I had not watched the shoemaker carefully enough when he repaired the shoed. I pleaded and tried to convince her that I had not taken my eyes off him even for an instant, but to no avail. The time soon approached for my brother to leave. Afterwards, my mother cried all night, fearing we would die from starvation. I tried suggesting that perhaps the diamond was in the other shoe, but she was inconsolable.

My brother worked in the same ammunitions factory as we, but in a different department. After his unsuccessful attempt to retrieve the diamond, he had to work the night shift. After eight hours of labor, he was marched back to his barrack under armed guards and attack dogs. He was hungry, exhausted, and very worried about my mother and the missing diamond. Upon reaching his barrack, he had to climb to his bunk, which happened to be on top. As he climbed up, the man sleeping in the bunk below called out, "Henry, be careful not to hurt yourself. You have a piece of something in your cuff."

Henry couldn't believe it. At first, he was so tired and exhausted he almost didn't pay attention to what the man below had said. Finally, though, he decided to take a quick look at his cuffs. To his great surprise, there was the diamond! He could not figure out how he came to have it, but he figured that he must have yanked so hard on the heel that the diamond popped out and fell into the cuff of his trousers without anyone even realizing it.

What a miracle! But he had no way to let our mother know. A day passed, but luckily he passed by her in the ammunitions factory and was able to whisper quickly to her that he had the diamond. My mother was overjoyed. She said to me, "This is a miracle. G-d wants me to have this diamond and pass it on to future generations" So she decided not to trade it for bread.

My mother carried this diamond through two ghettoes, Lodz and Szydlowiec; a slave labor camp; and two concentration camps, Auschwitz and Bergen-Belsen. After five long years, the war ended. Miraculously, we were still alive, though near death from starvation. A few days before the liberation, she was even unable to speak clearly. She said to me, "I am not going to make it. I want you to take the diamond and hide it." I began to cry and tried to encourage her, telling her that she must reach for the strength and determination to live for me. By the time we were liberated, she weighed forty-four pounds, and I weighed fifty-five. But she did survive.

My mother was sent to Switzerland, where she lived in a sanatorium for seven years until she regained her health. She remained in Switzerland afterwards for a total of seventeen years. She then came to the U.S.A. to be with us. Her children and grandchildren were the joy of her life. Here she wore the diamond ring with great pride and pleasure. It was the only item that remained of her pre-war possessions.

In time, my mother grew old and sick. She had cancer and did not last long. Before she passed away, she called me to her bedside and said to me, "My dear child, here is the diamond. Keep it, wear it, and pass it on to your oldest grandchild." When the time comes, I will fulfill her wish.

I have loved wearing the ring, and I always feel that my dear mother is with me when I wear it. However, its adventures were not yet over after my mother gave it to me. I almost never took it off my finger, but one day as I was preparing to leave for work and was finishing the dishes, I realized with a start that, even though the ring was on my hand, the diamond had fallen out of its setting. I almost fainted and didn't know what to do. My heart was broken. I started to cry, but I also began to pray. I begged G-d not to let me lose this precious diamond, the only thing left to me from our home. I was despondent. It was time to leave for work, but something inside me told me I had to look more and not give up. I looked everywhere in the room where I had been and searched all the corners. Suddenly, I saw something shining. I could not believe my eyes. I had found it. I was so grateful to G-d, and I began to cry and pray all at the same time, thinking, Yes, G-d is good to me.

I decided not to wear this mischievous diamond anymore. I had it repaired and then put it away so it would not be playing any tricks on me. I hope that my grandchildren and future generations will enjoy it and keep it in the family. I am sure that they will be able to read the stories about this diamond and will marvel at the miracles that have attended it.

THE FLOWER IN THE DEATH CAMP

I was sitting in the barrack, shivering from cold, hungry and thirsty. I was imagining how nice it would be to have something to eat. I looked outside the window. The sun was shining brightly, warming up the earth after a long and cold winter. There still were patches of melting snow. Because it was cold in the barrack, I decided to go outside to see if perhaps the sun could warm up my deteriorated and enfeebled body. I gathered up all my strength and energy and walked outside. I sat down on the steps and reflected that spring was on its way and we would not be so cold. You could feel spring in the air. A light breeze wafted by, and I even heard some birds singing. Maybe I was dreaming. The light, mold wind and the warm sun put me to sleep.

When I woke up and looked around, I realized once again that I was fenced in and imprisoned in a concentration camp, far from freedom and humanity. But, as I looked, all of a sudden I saw a tiny bit of green piercing through the snow. I wondered what it could be. To my great surprise, it was a little leaf with a flower bud. I could not believe my eyes. Here, where there was so much misery and death, here where people suffered so much, this little flower had pushed through the snow to get to the sunlight.

I watched the little flower grow every day. This tiny blossom was my secret. It gave me hope and determination and the will to survive. Finally, one day, the little blue blossom disappeared. But it had given me joy and hope and had brought a little beauty to my miserable life. I thought, My G-d, the world is beautiful in spite of everything. I will not give up hope.

I wanted so much to live. My world was small, but I still enjoyed little things. My body was like a walking skeleton, but my mind was clear. I could think what I wanted; nobody could read my thoughts. I could live in a world of my own. In a way, I was free at least to think as I wanted. I would survive, and I would tell the world what happened to six million Jews, because the world needs to know, and we must never let anyone hide the truth.

THE TRAGIC ESCAPE FROM THE LABOR CAMP

Shortly before World War II, the Polish government started to build huge ammunition factories. One of the facilities was located in the mall town of Wierzbrik. The name of this town was later changed to Starachowice. The factory was hidden on the outskirts of town, surrounded by large trees. It brought great prosperity to the town and its people, and many peasants left their farms and villages to move to the town and work. Jews were never allowed to work in government positions, but, even so, life improved for everyone in the town. New homes and businesses were constantly springing up, and people began to dress more nicely and take better care of themselves. Many Jews lived in this town, most of them poor, but they led quiet lives and were generally very religious. The men performed all sorts of work, and they benefited from the increased prosperity of the town. Many professions were closed to Jews, but they were still able to work as tailors, cobblers, and in various other trades.

World War II broke out in September 1939, and in no time the Germans had conquered Poland. This completely changed the lives of the townspeople, especially Jews. Many restrictions were imposed on the Jewish community, and ironically the Jews were now allowed to work in the ammunition factory—but as slave laborers without pay. All Jews were required to wear yellow stars on the front and back of their clothes. Later on, the Germans herded in more Jews from smaller towns and villages to augment the labor force. The town was now overcrowded, sometimes with seven or even more to a room, and suffering under unbelievable conditions. The Germans eventually formed a ghetto. Food was restricted, and epidemics broke out.

One day, the Germans surrounded the ghetto and made a selection. The young and healthy were allowed to remain and work; they others were sent to a concentration camp, where they were gassed and burned. Those who remained were placed in a fenced camp watched by guards with machine guns. The Jews were quartered in crowded barracks, without water or toilet facilities inside. Generally they were required to work seven days a week on a meager portion of soup and bread. Work breaks were very short, and many times after work the Germans would gather us in a large square where they had set up a gallows. We had to watch while they hanged or shor workers. They would then give us a warning. "You dirty Jews had better work hard, or you will be punished like these rats!" Exhausted from hard work and hunger, we were led to the barracks.

In the ammunition factory, we worked with Christians who were paid for their labor and lived in their own homes in the town. Some of them were very righteous people who stood up for justice, and they tried to help us. Some belonged to underground organizations and fought the Germans when they could. One day, the Christian workers tried to organize some of the young Jews and told them to escape from camp before the Germans killed them. The Christians supplied them with wire cutters they had smuggled in to cut the chain fences. They told these Jews to storm the gate and run into the woods, where partisans would help them. But it was not so. When the Jews tried to escape, most of them were gunned down. A few managed to escape to freedom. The next day, the Germans announced a role call. They drove us out of the barracks, hitting and beating us and yelling obscenities. They took us to where about 350 to 400 people were lying on the ground. Most were dead, but a few were still alive. Some were begging for help, some were saying that it is better to die than to live under such horrible conditions. Others were still trying to cling to life. It is impossible to describe the scene completely. We had to watch them for hours as they lay bleeding until all were dead. The Germans began to yell at us, "You dirty Jewish rats! You wanted to run away, but you must work until you all die.! They said that all who tried to escape had perished, but they were wrong. Some did survive the tragic escape, and one of them was my husband Jacob.

Hitler did not succeed in his desire to kill all the Jews. We rebuilt our lives, married, had children and grandchildren. We have contributed to the world, and we teach and speak about the tragedy. It is totally unbelievable what people are capable of doing to others. We want to try to make a better world.

Doctors Before and During the War

I was born and was raised and attended school in Lodz, Poland, the second largest city in the country. Three hundred thousand Jews lived in Lodz. It was a flourishing Jewish community. When the Germans invaded Poland, the country fell in no time. The Germans ordered the Jews to wear yellow Stars of David in front and back with the inscription "Jews." Then, after a few months, they established a ghetto and forced us to live there. My father was a successful businessman and employed quite a few people. Luckily we were smuggled out of the ghetto by a very fine Christian who was a former employee of my father. But my father had to remain behind because he had to turn over his business machines to the Germans, who later killed him.

My mother's parents used to live in a shtetl. My wonderful grandparents were well off. They had special permission to sell cigarettes and alcohol. They owned a brewery and an apartment building. It was rare that Jews were given those kinds of privileges.

My mother used to tell me stories about the shtetl. I loved so much to listen to her. Once she told me about healers, both folk doctors and trained doctors and dentists. She said that, when she was growing up, if someone fell ill, people would first try to cure the person with all sorts of home remedies. But, if someone became seriously ill, the person was taken by horse and wagon to the nearest town that had a practicing doctor. However, if someone broke an arm or leg, the person was taken to a man who was a healer, and he would set the bones together—the fact that some people limped later on did not seem to matter. Healing was not this man's main profession; he was a vegetable salesman and healed people on the side.

There was also another kind of healer, called a feldsher (a medical practitioner without full formal credentials), who generally cared for those who were financially well off. The feldsher in their shtetl was a man known as Avraham the Feldsher. He was not educated in the medical profession, but he had a special talent for working with various herbs, and he helped some people to get over their illnesses. The feldshers were actually barbers, and in front of their businesses hung two bronze signs. These plates served as certificates to announce that the man inside could heal people. The children of the shtetl loved to listen to the sounds of the plates rattling when the wind was blowing.

There were also other healing practitioners in the shtetl. There were dentists who used very primitive instruments. Mostly they just pulled teeth out and did not treat them. And there were midwives who helped deliver the babies of the community. Generally, they were very successful. They learned their profession through long years of experience. There was even a little hospital, but most of the time it was empty.

In the 1930's, there was a change for the better in the shtetl. A new doctor arrived, one who really was a trained physician. He even had an office devoted exclusively to the practice of medicine. Later on came another doctor, and after that came one more, my uncle, Dr. Leon Dyment. He had studied in Paris, having been sent there by my grandfather, who was a prominent citizen in the shtetl with liberal views and felt he wanted his sons to experience the broadening power of education abroad.

When my uncle began to practice medicine, the whole town was overjoyed. They not only had their own doctor, but one who had studied at the Sorbonne, which had a great reputation. He did not charge much for visits; most of the people were poor. He did not even ask for money. If a patient offered money, that was great, but if he were too poor, he even supplied their medicine for free. May G-d bless him. Often he would send food along with the medicine. He was an extraordinary human being.

With the outbreak of World War II, my uncle was mobilized as a high ranking officer of the Polish army. For a few weeks, we did not even know if he was still alive or had been killed. One day, he came home. He was a broken man. He had walked hundreds of miles. His uniform was in rags. We all were so glad to see him. By this time, all the Christian doctors had left town; they were forbidden to treat Jewish patients. My uncle was then practically the only healer left in a town with a growing population. The Germans had deported Jews from other towns and had formed a ghetto. We were forced to live with about ten people in two rooms. In the third room, my uncle opened an office. Six people stormed the door, begging for help. He felt helpless, but sometimes he managed to obtain some medicine from some doctors in France whom he knew.

This situation did not last long. The Gestapo ordered that a hospital be opened, so that they would know who was sick in order to send them to concentration camps for extermination. A few weeks later, they encircled the ghetto and deported most of the people to camps where they were gassed and burned in crematoria. Others they sent to slave labor camps, where they died from epidemics and starvation. My uncle, his wife Karola, and his son Artur were hidden by a Christian physician, Dr. Cimiega. They could have survived, but there were a lot of informers, and one of them informed the Gestapo. They came and found my aunt and uncle and took them away, but his son was saved because he was out with Dr. Cimiega's wife when the Gestapo came.

The Germans tortured my uncle and beat him terribly because they wanted to know where his son was. In order to avoid revealing where his son was hidden, my uncle committed suicide. His wife Karola was sent to Auschwitz. Mrs. Cimiega sent Artur out of town to live with a friend of hers. He survived the war undetected. His mother also survived Auschwitz and was reunited in Poland with her son after the war. They later moved to France, where Karola had family. Artur is now a professor of mathematics at the University of Lille, where he lives with his family. His mother although quite old, is still alive. Each time I write her a letter, I pray that I will receive an answer. Following the war, our family was contacted by my uncle's cell mate, who related to us the story of my uncle's courageous sacrifice. The former cell mate later wrote a book about their experiences.

I have many other stories about doctors and healers, but I will save those for another time. May the life I have recounted here be an example for others.

A TRIBUTE TO MY MOTHER

My mother, Sarah Wajchendler, was a Holocaust survivor. She endured two ghettoes, Lodz and Szydlowiec, and the Starachowice labor camp, the Hermann Goering ammunition factory and two concentration camps, Auschwitz and Bergen-Belsen. My mother survived by the grace of G-d; she went through persecution, misery, humiliation, starvation and terrible illness. Throughout her ordeal, her sustaining force was her deep devotion and her faith in G-d.

My mother's life personified love, sensitivity, kindness and profound commitment to her husband and children. Her warm smile lighted up so many people's lives. Her personality and concern touched so many hearts. To me and to many others, she imparted determination and encouragement, which helped us so much through those tragic times. She always wanted to give me her small share of bread and soup, saying, "Eat, eat, my child. I am not hungry at all. You are so young. You need to survive. Someday you will be able to tell people what happened to the Jews." At the time, she was thirty-eight years old. I would look at my Mom and start to cry. I said to her, "Mom, we will both survive together or die together. But we shouldn't talk like this. We are going to survive. That is G-d's will."

Her faith was so great that, when important holidays came up, she would trade her bread for a candle so that she could pray for a better tomorrow. Her kindness was so remarkable that once even our Kapo in the camp came up and asked, "You two, are you sisters or what?" I replied No, that we were mother and daughter, and from time to time the Kapo gave us an extra slice of bread, which was such a great help in those terribly hungry times.

I remember this Kapo. Her name was Mirale. She always told us about her mother and how she was not good to her but how she wished she could be alive with her. Time was so important. Each day, just to be alive was a great challenge.

My dear mother was well educated and wise. She never criticized, but rather tried to understand people. She respected others, and they respected her. She was a mother to so many whose mothers did not survive the concentration camps. Sometimes I was a little jealous because she paid so much attention to other girls, offering them courage, determination and love. She listened to them; they liked to speak about their mothers. Often they did not know what had happened to them, but they still hoped that someday they would be together again. How I wish I could have my mother now, but I realize that I was a lucky girl because I had her through the war and for a long time after.

After the war, my mother was very sick for a long time. She was sent to Switzerland from Germany. She spent several years in a sanatorium for tuberculosis. She was not expected to live, but, thanks to the remarkable care of the blessed Dr. Rollier, she made a seemingly miraculous recovery and came to this great country to join us. She took great pride in her grandchildren. They were the joy of her life.

She lived in St. Louis for some years, and then she became very sick, this time with cancer. She suffered debilitating pain, but she tried to keep the sweet smile on her face through it all so as not to trouble us. She died too young, but G-d had allowed her to live through the war and after to give so much of her goodness to others.

I miss her very much. She was not only my mother but my best friend, my mentor. I shall always remember her. She is inscribed in my heart with my fullest love and affection. She was always a Mensch, never too busy to listen to others. May her memory be blessed forever.

FAITH AND HOPE

Faith and hope are a very profound part of my life. They were and are in my heart, my soul and in my whole body.
I believed and still believe that there is a G-d and that He is there for all people and guides the world. As an individual person, I have a special relationship with Him and always have had.
This was particularly true during the tragic days of the Holocaust. Whatever befell, I always felt His presence.

I have always loved to observe nature, and I am filled with wonder as I behold the miracles of trees in full bloom with fruit to follow; birds chirping and chasing each other; the beautiful colors of butterflies and the buzzing of bees as they flutter from flower to flower to collect nectar for the queen; the cloudless blue sky with the sun shining brightly as it sends its rays to warm the earth and my exhausted body; the golden wheat bending to and fro in the light breeze; the rushing waters of rivers and streams; and the people and animals running in all directions. I am filled with awe as I contemplate the One who made this world. I feel a miraculous certainty that it was not I.

But I have also dreamed and thought of a different world, one where people will be good to themselves and to each other. Maybe tomorrow such a dream will come true. I have hoped and prayed that such a day would come. This vision was my secret comfort that helped me through the days of darkness.

FROM MARIA'S DAUGHTER JOANNE...

My mother was a young girl when the war started. She came from a very nice, upper-middle class family. Like so many other young Jewish women of that day, she was carefully taught moral lessons of how people should treat each other. No one prepared her for the horrors she experienced in the war. She learned survival lessons which you and I wouldn't even dream of in our worst nightmares. Besides herself, she helped save her brother and her mother from death many times.

After the war, she worked in a Jewish Community Center and an organization called UNR. UNR was a restitution organization, headed by Mrs. Steel, which helped displaced survivors to put their lives back together. After emigrating to the United States, both my parents did everything they could to help other refugees who came later.

My mother and my father have often take time out often to speak to various groups about the Holocaust. They have never been too busy to educate others about what happened. In spire of their horrible experience, they have managed to instill their love of life and laughter in me. May G-d bless them.

Joanne Szapszewicz-Scott

THE LIBERATION OF
BERGEN-BELSEN

Fifty years ago, on the fifteenth of April 1945, I was liberated by the British Army from the concentration camp Bergen-Belsen. Fifty years is a long time, a half century in a human life. To me it seems like it happened yesterday. It was a beautiful sunny day and the most memorable day of my life. It was the day my freedom and humanity were given back to me. I shall never forget.

I woke up that morning, and with great difficulty I arose. Weak from starvation, exhausted from the work, I looked around for someone to talk to. The silence was startling as I realized I was surrounded mostly by dead bodies of others with whom I had talked only the night before. I wondered it I was alive. I asked my mother, who had been asleep next to me, "Am I alive or dead?" She answered, "My dear child, dead people cannot talk." There were not enough people to carry out the corpses. The smell was excruciating. I took the last bit of strength I had to leave the barrack and go to the commissary, hoping to find anything to eat.

I dragged my feet, resting every few feet. My desperate desire to survive kept me going. As I neared the commissary I looked up incredulously at what I saw: a white flag waving on the roof. Some German soldiers passed by wearing white bands on their arms. They weren't carrying any guns or other weapons! I was overwhelmed. I quickly returned to the barrack to tell the women the good news. I told them, "Girls, we are free. The German soldiers are unarmed!"

They turned to me with blank stares, glassy-eyed and hopeless. They spat at me and said, "You are a dreamer and a liar. You are crazy to never give up hope!"

The Kapo (a supervisor, also Jewish) overheard our conversation. She was a young, well-fed woman. She yelled, "What did I hear you say? We are free? If you are lying, I'll make you as free as those corpses around us!"

I was terrified of a beating by her, so I replied, "Maybe I am imagining it."

The Kapo walked out to see for herself and ran back, crying, "She is telling the truth. We are liberated by the British Army." Even then, nobody believed her until some British soldiers walked into the barrack.

The soldiers were stunned by the picture before them. They discovered emaciated human shadows crawling among the corpses in the filthy, narrow barracks, a scene so haunting it would have to remain with them forever. They began to weep, saying this was worse than any battlefield they had seen.

"How can we help you? What can we do?"

"Water. We want water." We had not had any water for a few days.

I gathered my strength and walked outside. I saw more soldiers approaching the camp and men coming out of the men's barracks. Tears of joy and hope were everywhere. I broke down crying when I saw a fellow survivor bend down to kiss the dusty boots of a British soldier. He cried, "G-d bless you for liberating us and saving our lives. Another few days and all of us would be dead."

A GATHERING TO REMEMBER

Almost every year since coming to this great country from Poland, my family has tried to spend part of the winter in Florida, mostly in Miami Beach, so as to be near the ocean and take advantage of the sun and water and go for long walks. In recent years, my husband's sister has joined us, and this past year we had planned a small family reunion here. Our children--Rose, Joanne, her husband Gary and our two precious granddaughters Marisa and Ariéla--were also planning to join us in Florida. But our reunion was not meant to be. My husband's sister informed us that this year her health would not permit her to journey from her home in Germany to Florida. My heart was very heavy, and I felt so sorry for my husband, who loves his sister dearly. We decided to make the best of things and go to Florida anyway. My daughter Rose still planned to join us so she could help celebrate my approaching birthday in Florida, but our daughter Joanne and her family decided to postpone their trip so the children would not be taken out of school. I told my husband that we would make the best of our situation and try to enjoy our trip. Perhaps we would do some reading or meet some old friends or make some new ones.

One day, while returning from the beach, I heard a voice calling, "Madzia, Madzia!" (my nickname). "I knew that was you"!

I wondered who could possibly know my name. I turned my head and, to my surprise, a woman came up to me and said, "Madzia, don't you recognize me? I am Regina from Szydlowiec."

I looked at her and asked, "Do I know you?"

She replied, "You used to live in the Szydlowiec Ghetto." She then began to remind me of former times, and little by little I started to recall her. She said, "Madzia, do you know that you have many friends who remember you? They were with you in the ghetto and in the labor camp Starachowice, where we worked in the ammunition factory."

I was so happy to hear this. She went on, "I am going home and let my cousin know that you are here. And on February

26, there is going to be a gathering here in Miami of the survivors from the Starachowice labor camp. Those of us who are still alive [we are getting older every year, and time is running out] try to get together every year. Would you like to come?"

"My heavens," I replied. "I would be more than delighted to come and see you all. So often I have wondered about you for fifty years. You were all so dear to my heart!"

We parted with Regina assuring me that her cousin Hanna would know even more people who knew me. Within just a few days, the phone in our hotel room began to ring often. People I would even recognize today called to give me their names and reminisce about the past. So much had happened since then! We had married, had children and grandchildren and grown old.

I could hardly wait for the day of the gathering. The night before, my old friend Gitele Friedersohn called me, saying she would like to get together. We had so much in common. My gratitude goes out to her dear husband, who in Starowice tried to shield my mother from selection. May G-d bless them! They are such fine people, and their door is always open to survivors.

Finally, the day arrived. Out of excitement, I was unable to sleep the night before. It was to be a luncheon meeting, and, on the way over, my heart was beating rapidly. My only second cousin, Howard Chandler, who had also called me the night before, was there from Canada with his dear wife Elsa. I met so many people at the gathering whom I did not even know had survived. I even met a woman who had shared a bunk with me as a girl. I had a coat then, and during the cold nights it became our blanket. How we pulled on that coat, because it wasn't big enough to cover both of us! We were such good friends. Her maiden name was Basta Greenspan. I remember her so well; she saved my life and I saved her life, but those stories are too long to tell here. She was beautiful then and still is.

Some ladies came up to me who had been close friends in the camp and later on in the displaced persons' camp as well. We had lost touch, what with everyone trying to adjust to a new life, which was not easy. We were alone; Poland, our homeland, did not claim us; they did not want us. They now owned our family properties and did not want to give them up.

I had a conversation with my dear friend Irka Schacter and her sister Rachela. Irka remembered my dear brother Lolek, who perished in Mauthausen near the end of the war. Those terrible German beasts had given him a gas shot in his heart. It hurt me so much—I was already liberated from Bergen-Belsen and was hoping that he would survive too. Irka said to me, "Your brother was such a nice boy. He was very young. He helped me to carry the huge bullets to the machine. I could never forget how good and kind he was to me." During those tragic times, the best and the worst came out of people.

We had a delicious lunch and were entertained by an Israeli singer as we ate. We then heard some speeches by survivors, and I had the great honor and privilege to read an article I had written about my mother. My mother had survived the war, and this article was a tribute to her and to the mothers who did not survive. I was so excited that I was crying from joy to see those people who had shared with me the worse of tragedies in human history. I was so pleased and happy to see them vibrant, healthy and successful, despite our age! I was so grateful to G-d that we had all made it and could gather together to share our memories and talk about those friends who didn't survive We recited Kaddish on their behalf.

May G-d bless all my dear friends and their families with good health and happiness, and I shall say, "Hazak, ayis hazak. Let us be strong and strengthen ourselves. Long live Israel, our beloved country. Am Yisrael chai!"

REPORT FROM ST. LOUIS

The *Together* magazine had just arrived. Pictures from the past began to swirl across my mind like images in a kaleidoscope as I began to read. I am a Holocaust survivor. I withstood two ghettoes, a labor camp, Auschwitz and Bergen-Belsen, where I was liberated by the British army. Turning the pages of the magazine, I recognized many familiar names, including Sam Bloch and Dr. Bimko, the mother of Menachem Rosensaft. Menachem perhaps doesn't realize just how much his father—may his name be blessed—did for survivors. I shall always remember him. When my mother, who survived along with one of my two brothers, suffered from advanced tuberculosis following the war, Mr. Rosensaft arranged for her to be sent to a sanitarium in Switzerland. Thanks to his caring, she was able to make a complete recovery. In 1960, she joined us in the Unites States. All survivors lost a great friend when Mr. Rosensaft passed away. His family should be justifiably proud of this fine and humble person.

I live in St. Louis, whose population includes about fifty thousand Jews. It is a wonderful, vibrant community where people care about and assist one another. About two years ago, thanks to the generosity of the people and the Jewish Federation, we built a beautiful Holocaust Museum and Learning Center. About one hundred survivors and their families now inhabit St. Louis. There once were more, but many have died.

We want everyone to know how much we value our Museum. We retain close to sixty docents, of whom only a few are survivors (not all survivors are able to talk about such horrible experiences). We work very hard giving lectures and speeches in schools and universities, showing videos and presenting monthly films concerning the Holocaust. We often travel out of town to speak at churches in smaller communities. Nothing is too difficult for us; we want the world to know what happened to six million Jews, one and a half million of which were children.

The responses from our audiences have been tremendous. Some people had never met a Jew. These people are especially thankful for providing them with such a unique learning experience. I wish I could show everyone the beautiful letters I have received. I feel that it is our duty and obligation to provide this information for those who cannot speak. This is our tribute to them.

The Holocaust Museum and Learning Center is dedicated mostly to survivors who live in St. Louis, and it is particularly moving because visitors are able to hear eyewitness accounts directly from survivors there. In many cases, they can also view pictures of us and our families from before and after the war. Many exhibits show how the Jews lived and flourished before the war and then after the liberation.

The Museum has several rooms. An introductory room displays pictures of our families and ourselves. The second room presents a panorama of Jewish life before the war, consisting of religious artifacts, pictures, videos, maps, and charts detailing the rise of Nazism. The third room documents the Holocaust during 1939-45, presenting pictures of ghettoes, slave labor camps, Jewish resistance and medical experiments performed by German doctors. Also displayed is a very large model of the Lodz Ghetto, pictures of the Warsaw Ghetto uprising, and audio presentations by survivors. The fourth room shows pictures of deportations, selections, and death marches.

Upon moving to the fifth and sixth rooms, one sees pictures of our rescuers, the Nuremberg trials, and Jewish life in displaced persons camps after the war. Perhaps most significant of all is the collection of photographs of the birth of our beloved country, Israel. The final room is a large auditorium where films and videos are shown and lectures delivered.

As a docent for the museum, I pledge that there will always be someone to speak about those who perished. I am very grateful to the Jewish Federation, which gave us so much to be proud of in our great Holocaust Museum and Learning Center. Thousands of people have already learned about the Jewish tragedy during the

Nazi regime, and thousands more are yet to come. But perhaps, more importantly, all will learn that Jews will not perish. We will live, flourish and build new lives for ourselves and for Israel.

THE FIRST BIRTHDAY OF THE
HOLOCAUST MUSEUM AND LEARNING CENTER

The Holocaust Museum and Learning Center in St. Louis, Missouri has existed for one year. It is hard to believe that time flows so quickly, especially for us survivors, for whom time is so precious. During the period of the Nazi terror, a moment could mean life or death. We who value life so much take pride and satisfaction in the thought that we leave a living memorial to those who were murdered. Hitler did not survive, and his Final Solution did not work. We are here to tell the world of his horrible atrocities. I cannot understand why so few people tried to rescue the Jews; we are people like others, and we have always lived in peace as good and obedient citizens. And what about our wonderful children? Where were mercy and ethics at that time? And where were the clergy, who talk so much about brotherhood and love? Where were they when G-d's people were being hunted down? Believe me, humanity is the poorer for those great souls who perished. Who knows what any one of them might have contributed to humanity. But, thanks to G-d, we have this wonderful museum to help tell our story. This museum was my dream for many years, and I am so thankful that G-d allowed me to live to see it become a reality. This museum teaches young and old what happened and what people are capable of doing to others.

This museum was built thanks to generous support from individual donors and the Jewish Federation. We survivors are very thankful to them, and we salute them. This is a memorial to our mothers, our fathers, our children and our wonderful families and friends. I am a docent at the museum, and, each time I lead a group on a tour, I feel as if I am once again walking through the valley of death. But I know that the victims did not perish completely. I remember them; they have a life in my memory, and I will see that others know about them. I am especially happy about that.

When I lead a tour, I begin with a video that shows how the Jews lived before the war, how we survived and flourished together. Regardless of our individual experiences, we were all Jews sharing a common belief in G-d. In the video room, we have arti-facts, photographs from before the war, maps, and testimonies of survivors living in St. Louis. There is a beautiful painting of a Pol-ish synagogue. It is a wonderful piece of art, and I reflect upon the great talent that G-d bestowed on the artist--who knows, perhaps he is still alive--but his art lives forever. There is also a chronologi-cal map of Jewish history throughout the centuries. We learn that Jews were persecuted so many times, but we always survived, even after our enemies had turned to dust.

There are other rooms in the museum documenting the rise of Nazism, the book burnings, the persecutions, Kristallnacht and other persecutions performed by the so-called superior race. In one room is a model of the Lodz Ghetto and the Warsaw Ghetto with testimony from survivors. And we did not forget those brave freedom fighters, many of whom perished horribly, who took up arms against the Germans. G-d bless these brave men and women. We have a theater where we see films and pictures of the Final So-lution. And we remember those righteous Christians who risked their own lives to help us survive. May G-d bless them, too.

There are other rooms where visitors can see photographs of deportations, the methods of destruction, the Nuremberg tri-als, the liberation, more testimonies from survivors, and scenes of displaced persons camps after the war. Then the story of the birth of the modern state of Israel is depicted, the great miracle which emerged from our sufferings.

It would be impossible to encapsulate the whole museum in one article. On the contrary, this was not my purpose. I want you to come and see and learn. I pray that we can all learn how to respect each other and live together in peace. The Land of Israel and the Jewish people are a beacon of hope and light to the whole world, particularly to the poor and the oppressed. *L'chaim!*

FIFTY YEARS LATER

Fifty years after World War II, fifty years of life after the Holocaust liberation. We Holocaust survivors thought that the world would carry us on its shoulders, but it was not to be so. The end of the war was not that easy. We were mentally and physically exhausted, and we had no one to whom we could turn. We had lost our families, our possessions, and we were all sick in body. So many of us died after the war. We could not return to the cities, the shtetls, the settlements, most of which were in ruins. Almost everything had vanished. There were only cemeteries, and those had been vandalized. We were turned way by the countries in which we were born and where our ancestors had lived for centuries. We could not even go to Palestine, because the British government would not let us in. Some attempted to enter illegally—and some succeeded—but most were brought back to Germany and ended up in camps under British supervision. We survivors demonstrated and showed our solidarity with the passengers of the Exodus.

Bergen-Belsen had the largest population of survivors, and, with the help of the Jewish Brigade, it was out of this camp that the first emigrants left for Palestine. Many of us remained in resettlement camps for a few years after the war. Then other countries began to open their borders to us. Many of us left for the United States of America, the great country that took us in like a mother tending to weak and sick orphans, like the woman in Emma Lazarus' famous poem. At first, we knew very little about America. We could not speak the language and were unfamiliar with the culture and traditions. But this country gave us the opportunity to rebuild our lives, to start again from the beginning, to live in freedom as human beings.

Because of our immense determination, it is amazing what we accomplished. Like the mythical Phoenix, we rose from the ashes. We gave our children the precious things all children should have: love, warmth, compassion and respect for all other people regardless of their race or religion. We gave them the basics, and our children have built upon the seeds we planted and have contributed in great and significant ways to the country which gives freedom and dignity. Our children are famous doctors, lawyers, fighters for human rights and hard-working ordinary people. We salute the U.S.A., our great country. G-d bless "America the beautiful."

Yes, it has been fifty years, a half century. We survivors recently celebrated at a gathering in Miami. Four thousand Jews came to show unity and our liberators and Israel. The gathering took place at the Hotel Fontainebleau in Miami Beach. The large hotel reserved a special hall for us and named it "The Village," and to this hall, hundreds of survivors came and paced, looking and still hoping to find someone they knew or someone who knew about the fate of their loved ones.

We survivors will not surrender hope; we put up a board where people placed the names of their beloved. I hope that some were successful at finding a long-lost friend or loved one. One entire room was set up with tables representing countries, cities and shtetls. On the walls of the room were photographs of entire families; there were computers available and places where you could register your name. People were so kind and helpful. Our family was unable to find any of those we sought, but just being there was a priceless experience. There were all kinds of activities, speeches by survivors and dignitaries, music by the military band and festive dinners. On the morning of the last day, we marched to the Holocaust Memorial Center. It is one of the most touching places I know The Memorial consists of colonnades with panels depicting scenes from the concentration camps. In the middle stands an imposing sculpture with an outstretched hand reaching to Heaven. On the hand and arm are carved the figures of people reaching to freedom. Beside the statue is a memorial wall, a sad reminder of lost lives, with a list of names submitted by survivors. We prayed in silence and sang songs and recited the Kaddish. The cantor and the rabbi recited the "El Mole Rachim." And all of us wept for our family members who lost their lives during the horrid

Nazi regime.

After the gathering, people left for their various destinations. I felt such a terrible pain in my heart, thinking, "My G-d, we are getting so old; we are the last of the Mohicans. Is this our last hurrah?" I hope not, and I am sure our children will not forget our story. Let us always remember our fallen comrades, our families, and their lives and deaths, their struggles in the ghettoes and concentration camps, and their battles in the forests. They suffered hideously at the hands of German murderers and their helpers. Let us never forget the six million.

Am Israel chai!

INTERVIEW FOR THE SOUND ARCHIVE OF THE
IMPERIAL WAR MUSEUM, LONDON, ON AN EVENING IN 1997

[Note: The editor initially transcribed this interview in its entirety, subsequently shortened it slightly, and has standardized and formalized the syntax in order to assist the reading of it as a written document.]

Interviewer: Maria, could I ask you first of all to tell me about your background and your family.

Maria: I had a very loving family—my mother, my father and two brothers—and we lived very comfortably before the war. My father was a very successful businessman. My parents were educated people; they believed in education. We went to the best private schools. They always told us, "People can take everything away from you, but what you have inside—what you know—nobody can take away from you. They can only take it if they take away your life. Besides your health, this is the most valuable thing you have."

My parents were Jewish, and they were religious. They were also very progressive people. They believed in G-d, and my father, a very charitable man, went to the temple every Friday night.

Most Jews in Poland before the war were very poor. Maybe they didn't speak Polish well, but they were educated in the Torah, Talmud, and Mishna. The Jewish children went to school, called a cheder, starting at the age of three. They could not read or write, but they memorized

And I'll tell you a story. My husband is extremely brilliant and has three degrees. He has a photographic memory; he remembers everything. He told me stories from when he was a very little boy about three years old. They lived in a village and owned a huge farm with a mill and a large lake. They had quarries, and they had something like a factory where stones were cut for cemetery monuments. When he was a little boy, it was hard for them to get to school. On Friday night, his father was teaching the older brothers about the Torah, Chmish, Mishna, and Talmud. My husband was just listening. When next Friday night came, his father asked them to repeat what he taught them all week, and some of them didn't remember. My husband Jacob said, "Dad, Dad, I know." His father said, "You don't know anything. You be quiet." But he insisted that he knew. His mother said, "Let him tell you what he knows." To everyone's surprise, he repeated exactly what his father had taught the older boys.

I: Could I ask you about your village? What was the name of it?

M: I did not live in a village. I lived in a beautiful city, Lodz, the second largest city in Poland after the capital. It had a population of about a million people before the war: three hundred thousand Jews and about two hundred and fifty thousand Germans. We were all Polish citizens. But, when the war broke out, although the Jews were Polish citizens, the ethnic Germans, because they were full-fledged Germans, enlisted in the army; they became guards in ghettos and camps. They were informers, and there were very few nice people among them.

I: Did you experience any anti-Semitism before the war?

M: Yes, I did. I took French lessons with my girlfriend. We had to walk maybe ten blocks to our teacher, Professor Axelrod, and on our way back home little boys used to shout, "Jew, Jew, Jew." We were just two girls, so we started to run, and I remember there was a big yard and a dilapidated movie theatre, and we tried to get in as they chased us. They started to beat us up, and they scratched my face. When I came home, our housekeeper looked at me and said, "What happened to you?" I said, "Nothing," because I didn't want my mother to know and to worry. But she said, "Tell me." She was a Christian, a very righteous woman, and she said to me, "What happened to you? Why don't you tell me?" I started to cry, and I told her. She was very upset and very sorry about it, and she said, "I will hurry up with the work, and I'll make sure I will take you to those lessons."

I had other experiences, too. Poland was a very anti-Semitic country; the majority hated the Jews. Most of the people didn't stand up for the Jews—only very few did. I don't know why. Many times I asked, "Why do they hate us so much? I didn't do anything." There were righteous people, but not too many.

I had a lot of experiences. I remember once going to a food store with my Mom, and my Mom asked for grapes, but the box had just single grapes. My Mom asked, "Please give me a bunch." The woman behind the counter said, "Don't you know! They have to have the best!" And my Mom said to her, "Look. I pay for good food, not for food that is not good." But the lady who owned the store knew my Mom and knew us. She said, "Please don't make anything out of it." Though a little girl, I distinctly remember that.

I: Did you have any brothers or sisters.

M: I have two brothers. My older brother's name was Henry Wajchendler. The younger brother, Leon, tragically perished at Mauthausen. I was liberated April 15, 1945 by the British Army. About the 18th or 20th of April, the Nazis put a shot of gasoline in my brother's heart. It was more painful because I was already enjoying liberty.

I: The German invasion, do you remember that?

M: Yes, distinctly. As I mentioned, we had a very nice life, and it was the first of Sept. 1939 when the Germans invaded Poland. It didn't take long; after three days, they came to my town. The first thing they did was burned synagogues. They took out the Torahs, they took out the books, and they put them in the square. One whole group of German soldiers were laughing, and the other ones put the Torah and other books in the fire. The burning of books hurt me very much because, you know, books are like the soul of a human being. I remember this occurrence distinctly; I remember it so well.

I like to read a lot, and I had a book about the Inquisition in Spain —maybe you're familiar with it, since you're a history professor. The author's name was Leo Feuchtfanger. It was a beautiful book about what the Spaniards did to the Jews during the Inquisition. The name of the book was—I am translating from Polish into English—The Jewish Woman from Toledo. When I read it aloud to my father, I couldn't believe the cruel way people treated each other. I said, "Look how the writer exaggerated. How can he exaggerate like this!" And my father looked at me. He said, "Please give me the book; we're not supposed to have this book. This book is forbidden; they burned those books." And I said, "Dad, I would like to finish." Then he said, "It's not exaggerated. That's the way it really was." I did not know what was waiting for me.

My first encounter occurred one day when the Germans burst into our house. I had a beautiful little dog, a poodle which started to bark because these intruders were not familiar people. They instantly shot my dog, and I started to cry terribly. My father said, "Stop it. Quiet. Stop it. They will kill us if you will carry on like this." I loved that little dog, and this was my first encounter with death.

When the Germans arrived, they gathered up the Jews and made fun of them; they cut their beards to the skin, and blood was running. Once I wanted to visit my girlfriend, and my father said, "No, you cannot go." I said, "Dad, she lives just three houses away, and I haven't been out for so many days." I begged him, and he said, "All right, but come back as soon as possible." That's when I saw the Germans mistreating the Jews. I was so frightened, I didn't even visit her; I came home, and I cried terribly.

I: Were you made to wear the yellow star?

M: After a few days, a decree came out that all the Jewish people had to wear a yellow star, though, actually, in Lodz we did not wear yellow stars; we wore a band with a blue star because, you see, there were a lot of Germans living there, and Poland was divided. Part of Poland belonged to the Germans. The name of the town was Lodz, but they changed that name to Litzmannstadt in honor of the German general Litzmann, who conquered Lodz before the First World War.

I had a wonderful family. I had cousins, uncles and aunts, and we were a very close-knit family. Before the war, Jewish people had a lot of children. The more educated didn't have as many— usually two or three at the most—but others had a lot of children. While the father studied the Torah and taught the boys, the mother and the older children went to work. That's how it was. Maybe a half year later, in April, they formed a ghetto in Lodz. In the beginning, we didn't have it so bad. Though food was restricted, we stored some food because we were afraid that the war would break out and we wouldn't have enough food, but we didn't have enough food to last a long time. And besides, since my father was in business, he imported some goods like factory machines from Germany and from other countries. He had to deliver our goods to the Germans because they melted them and made weapons out of them later.

My father was a businessman, and the Germans made him a "Treuhandler," giving him permission to go out under guard and to deliver our goods to the Germans. He used to have two green bands; these showed that he was Jewish and had permission to go out. He was freer than we were. Sometimes he had some friends, people who worked for us before the war, who brought some bread which he put in his pocket. So it was bad, but not as bad as for others.

At the end of March, some Germans burst into our apartment and started to shout, "Out! Out! Out!" They put all the Jews in one place, and they started to drive us into the ghetto, the most deteriorated part of the city. Only extremely poor people lived there who lacked bread and didn't have enough food. This part of the city deteriorated; there weren't apartments with two bedrooms or one bedroom and a kitchen; there was only one room, and in the middle of the room was a stove with one burner and a pipe. They had to burn coal or wood, and we had to live there with another family.

The way the Germans chased us, we had to leave our homes quickly. We couldn't take much with us, because we didn't have the means. Some people had little children's carriages, and they put their things in them to push. If the older people couldn't get out fast enough from their apartments, the Germans killed them, even the little children. We also had to run because the Germans came on bikes with huge dogs. If somebody fell, the dogs bit the people, and then others fell over them because they were carrying something heavy. They didn't have much strength, and they dropped the little suitcases or whatever they had, others fell on them, and the guards shot them for their enjoyment. We were fenced into the Lodz Ghetto. Our food was rationed; we had nine hundred calories a day per grownup; little children didn't get anything. Everybody had to work, starting from about the age of nine or ten.

I: What did you do?

M: They taught me how to sew. I was not in the Lodz Ghetto long—only about a year. I was smuggled out of the ghetto. My father had permission to go in and out of the ghetto every day because he had to deliver the goods, the machines, so he smuggled in some bread. Going in and out every day, he got to know the guards, the Germans, and he may have bribed them sometimes. I don't know.

It's remarkable that we had school in the beginning, but not for long. They probably took the older girls to work; we didn't know what happened to them.

Then we had underground schools with very devoted teachers. We also had a theater for a short time, and I also used to go with my Mom to the symphony.

In the ghetto where we lived, the water was outside in the courtyard, and the toilet was also outside. Inside the room, we didn't have any running water nor a toilet. I remember one day that I woke up and wanted to go to the bathroom. I quickly came back, and I started to cry. My Mom said, "Why are you crying so?" I said, "Come with me! Look what happened!" The people had completely dismantled the wooden stairs because it was very cold and they didn't have anything to burn in the stove. But we were young; we found a way to get out. On top of the steps was wood; underneath was cement. We got by.

We had a manager; he was the most wonderful human being, such a great man. This Mr. Kurtkowsky told my father, "I have to save the children. I would like to save your wife, too." And my father said, "How can you do it?" And he said, "Look, we've known each other a long time. I worked for you, and you've always been very good to me. I have a way." My father said, "What way. Tell me!" He said, "My very distant relative is a guard. He is a German, but I told him I would give him money. He will just turn his head the other way and will get us out." My father was very frightened, and I overheard him telling this to my mom, who started to cry. She said, "I don't want to leave you alone." But my father insisted, saying, "That's the only chance we have." We didn't know what was waiting for us. He took us out the next day, and we traveled about five days by carriage—always at night, because during the daytime we were hiding. We had those bands with the star, and we always covered them so the Germans couldn't detect us.

I have grandparents who lived in a little town, a shtetl,

where about ninety percent of the town's population was Jewish. The name of this place was Szydlowiec. My Mom was born in this little town, but, when she married, they went to the big city Lodz because my father's parents lived in there. So we traveled a long time.

My grandparents were well off; they had a few apartment buildings. These were not high-rise buildings, just about three-stories high. They used to own a brewery, too. We went often for vacation to visit them because they had dogs, so many cats, and horses and carriage. We didn't have this in the big city, just a little dog. We loved going there.

My grandfather was a very generous man; he always wanted to give us the best, and he did. They died before the war. My grandfather was a very liberal man who believed in education. They had three sons and four daughters. My Mom was the oldest, and he educated all the children. My Mom graduated from the high school, the Gymnasium. Before the war, one usually went to public school, and that was the end of one's education.

My grandpa believed in education, so he sent his sons out of the country. My older uncle graduated from the Sorbonne in medicine before the war. The other son went to Liege in Belgium and became a chemical engineer. My grandpa was sick; his wife (my grandma) died, and it was very costly to send children abroad for education. So my uncle said to his brother, "You'll have to go to school here in Poland. You must go to Warsaw and apply." And, since he was an excellent student and had graduated from high school, he applied. But he suffered terrible anti-Semitic experiences and was treated like a numerus nullus. So he went to school, and, during the war, quite often he told us that they beat him up. He had to sit in the auditorium on the last bench and then walk out last after the others left. Two students were standing at the door pushing him, and he just ignored them because, if he had started a fight, he said they might kill him or beat him up, and he would never be right; they would always be right.

I: The shtetl where your grandparents had lived, was that then a ghetto area?

M: In the beginning, the Jewish people lived in a shtetl, but it was not fenced as in the larger ghetto. There were restrictions about where and when we could walk. When we came to this little shtetl, my two uncles (the doctor and the other one, who graduated in medicine but hadn't interned) were already there, as well as the third uncle. "How did you get out of the ghetto?" they asked. And the man who smuggled us out told them, "It's unbelievable! Oh, G-d, it's unbelievable!" There were housing restrictions on how many rooms you could have; they had about three rooms where three families lived. And this is where we came.

All the Christian doctors had left the town because they were not allowed to treat Jewish patients. After they had put all the Jews from the smaller towns and villages into this shtetl, it swelled from ten thousand people to about thirty thousand people. There was no doctor, so my uncles started to practice medicine, but they didn't have a place to work, so they decided to use one room as a clinic, and they asked me to be their receptionist.

There was a terrible epidemic of typhus because, as in the larger ghetto, people didn't have facilities where they could wash or go to the toilet. Every day, people were dying by the dozens. In addition, we didn't have any transportation in the ghetto; there was only one fire truck. Almost everything was done by hand. They collected the dead bodies manually; they put them on a cart. In the beginning, we were strong, and we took the dead bodies to the cemetery to bury, but, when people became weak and sick, they put the bodies outside where designated people collected and buried them in a common grave. Because we did not have horses in the ghetto, some people were pushing or pulling the carts. I could show you pictures in our Holocaust Museum which were taken by the Germans to send home to show their families what great heroes they were in waging a war against children and adults.

I: Was this shtetl enclosed eventually, or was it still open when the other people came?

M: Though it was not fenced in, where you could and could not walk was restricted, and, if you disobeyed, you were punished. I remember that I was the receptionist, and they made an office out of one room where they examined the sick people, but they didn't have any medication during this horrible, horrible epidemic of typhus, and people were dying on the streets. I remember distinctly one of my uncles lamenting, "What can I do for those people?" The younger one said, "All we can give them is hope, nothing else. Let's tell them the war will soon be over. Just keep on going and tell them, 'You are not so sick; it's not that bad. Just wash yourself and take care of yourself.'" And that was the medication they gave out.

I: Could you tell me how typhus affects people?

M: Typhus is a horrible sickness. It's a disease of the blood in which you get a very high fever, as high as 106° F, which dehydrates your body and makes you constantly want water. You get red spots, you are inflamed, you cannot talk, and it affects your eyesight. I remember thousands of people dying from typhus. I was in two ghettoes, one labor camp, and two concentration camps; there was a terrible epidemic in the labor camp.

I: Speaking of the place where you are at the moment in the shtetl, weren't the Germans rather worried about the typhus?

M: They were indeed aware of typhus, and they didn't come into the ghetto; they just watched the people from the outside. They guarded but didn't come into the ghetto.

During the regime of Marshal Pétain, my uncle, who had graduated from the Sorbonne, started to treat the people with words of hope. He had many doctor friends with whom he was in touch before the war. He wrote a letter asking them to send shots against typhus, and, believe it or not, he got a package of perhaps a hundred. He told me, "You need going to get a shot because you handle the public." He got a shot, and he gave my whole family an injection, except my Mom, who was sick and didn't want one. She almost died in the labor camp.

As I mentioned, there weren't any Christian doctors. And, because the nearby Christian villagers, the peasants, didn't have a doctor when they got sick, they risked their lives and came to my uncle for treatment. The peasants could get some medications from drug stores, but not everything they needed. At night, quite often, they stormed the very heavy city gates of this fifteenth-century shtetl. Because so many came, we couldn't sleep at night. My uncle treated them, and they brought some chickens, eggs, and so forth, because they were free people who could farm their land. They did have to give some of their produce to the Germans, but they didn't declare everything, and my uncle got some of it. They brought some cheese and some butter—not much—but it was good.

We had a maid, a Jewish woman, who just worked to get a little bit more food. We had soup made from one of the chickens from the peasants, and my uncle said to her, "Why don't you take this chicken soup?" We also still had a cellar where we had wines of all kinds. He said, "Take a bottle of red wine." My uncle was a very good-hearted human being. His wife is still living in Paris at ninety-three years old. She told her husband, "It's not enough that you don't take any money. You give away our food!" He answered, "The Christians are still coming, and I will risk my life to treat them. Don't worry." That's the way we shared our food. We didn't have enough, but we were not as hungry as others were.

One day, the Germans circled the whole ghetto with their

huge trucks and tanks. They gathered all the Jews and started a selection, and my Mom was with us. My father had wanted to get out of the ghetto because some Christians had told him, "They're going to take the green band away from you because there is not much to deliver any more." The Germans shot and killed him.

The Germans gathered together all the Jews in this little shtetl for the selection and started to shout, "This side! Go on this side! Go on this side!" Because we thought of her as old, although she was actually only about thirty-eight years old, we were scared that they would select my Mom to die. We were so scared. My brothers and I looked and looked, and we finally found her and took her with us. I also saw young people who didn't want to give up their children.

I had an aunt whose name was Sophie, and this incident will always remain in my heart, mind, and before my eyes. She was the wife of my uncle who went to Liege and graduated in chemistry. They had a little child, three years old, and she carried this child. During the selection, the Nazis pushed her to the side to die. My uncle said to her, "Sophie, Sophie, leave him! Come on this side. You are young." She was about twenty-four years old and was a beautiful woman. We didn't believe that they were going to put us in Auschwitz and gas us and burn us in crematoriums. He said, "We'll make another life," and she was almost ready to leave her child. She moved, and this little boy, my cousin Chilus, wouldn't let her go. Then she took him in her arms, and she started to hug him and kiss him, and she said to her husband, "There's no way I am going without him."

And they took those of us who looked better, who were in better health and more fit. They put us on trains and took us to a town called Starachowice, where the HermannGoeringswerke, an ammunition factory, stood, and they gave us little green cards stating we had to work in that factory every day; there were three shifts. When we got off the trains, we asked, "Where are we going to live?" You could not imagine how crowded the shtetl was; people were living ten to twelve in one room, and everybody wanted to get out and breathe fresh air. My Mom started to cry. She said, "What am I going to do with three children? What am I going to do? I don't have any place decent to live." We also wept, we were so hungry.

All of a sudden, she blurted out, "Oh, my G-d. I think I have a distant cousin here, a really distant relative." I said, "What's his name?" She answered, "I've never been in touch with him. I only heard about him from my mother." We said, "Mommy, don't you know his name? How could you not know?" But she said simply, "I don't know his name." We started to guess, naming this name and that name. We kept coming up with names, each time saying, "I think that's the name." She finally said to us, "Children, each of you should take up a different position and ask everybody who passes by." And, standing up hungry, starved, and exhausted, we did this. Suddenly, a man said, "I know the person you're asking about. He lives near here." My Mom asked him to take us there, which he did. The man he took us to was standing at his door and said, "What do you want?" My Mom said, "I'm your relative. Won't you let me in?" He looked at her and said, "Now I have a hundred relatives, and everybody wants to get in. I cannot take you in; I have maybe thirty people in these two rooms. I'm not going to take you in. Go away!" My Mom started to cry, and we cried with her. We cried and cried and didn't want to move, but suddenly he felt sorry and said, "All right. Get in, if you can find a place, but you won't find a place." As a matter of fact, we couldn't find a place to lie down, but it was a relief to have a place to sit, and at least we had a roof over our heads. Then we had to walk to the factory, and we had to wear some sort of tag so the Christians could tell that we were Jews by our yellow star. We walked to the factory and worked about eight or nine hours.

I: What was the work that you did, Maria?

M: I was cleaning huge bullets for machine guns. I didn't know how, because I was not used to working in a factory, but there were Christians who worked in this factory. They were free people; they came to work, they got paid, and they went home. Some of them were very righteous, wonderful human beings. They helped us and showed us what to do; when the Germans guards were not watching, they showed us how to do the work. They also kept us informed about what was going on in the world. They belonged to all kinds of underground organizations, and they had radios hidden, though I didn't know where. They knew what was going on, and they told us. We walked from this shtetl towards the outskirts where the factory was—it was hidden in a wooded area because the Germans feared the airplane raids. So we walked and walked; it was about four or five miles.

And one day they gathered the whole shtetl together again and put a lot of guards around the shtetl so nobody could escape. Then, they started to select people. This time, my Mom was in the factory, and we had a very nice German man who was in charge of our department. He liked to get paid—to be bribed—for what he did. And he needed the people to work, and, when he heard that there was a selection in the shtetl, he wouldn't let them go back to the shtetl but kept them in the factory. My Mom was working on that shift. I was young, and I and my brothers had our passes. They put us on one side; and, on the other side, they put the other people who did not work and their children, even young people. These they put on cattle cars to send to Auschwitz, where they would be gassed and burned in the crematoriums.

We worked in that factory about a year and a half. And there was an unbelievably terrible epidemic of typhus. We had it bad, but not as bad as others, because at least we worked with very nice people who shared their lunches with us. Otherwise, our food consisted only of a very thin soup—I don't know if it was coffee; it was a dark, warm water—and a slice of bread. And when we came to the factory, they gave us more soup. So, these kind people shared their lunch with us. We were nearly starved to death from hunger.

One day, they put us all in a camp which they had built; it contained bunk beds. This camp was fenced in, and there were guards at the gates. They separated the men and women, and every day, when they woke us up, they counted us. And we had to walk about four or five miles to the factory under supervision of guards with dogs. I worked with my Mom, and I continued to have hope. One day when a cat went by, I said, "Oh, Mom, look at the cat. I want to be a cat." She said, "A cat? Why a cat?" I said, "Mom, I'd like either to be a bird who is free to fly or to be a cat who is free to run around. I want to be free." And she said, "Be what you are, my dear child. Maybe the war won't last long." We had hope, but it was bad in this camp. Our water source was outside; the toilet was outside—it was just a pool with a ditch; and people were dying from the horrible typhus epidemic. Although I often talk about this in the Holocaust Museum in St. Louis where I'm a docent, you cannot tell in an hour and a half what happened during five years.

I remember that one day my finger got infected, and there was no medication and no doctor in the camp. Like me, the doctors who were there had to work; there was perhaps a single doctor reserved for the mighty and privileged. I was in terrible pain. There wasn't any antiseptic or a bandage, so I tore a piece of my dress and wrapped it around my finger. I couldn't work, but I still had to go to work. I cried all night, and I couldn't sleep. In the morning, when I woke up, I was still crying from the terrible pain, and there was a lot of pus in the finger. My Mom saw that I had a red stripe and suddenly said, "My G-d! My G-d!" That's gangrene!" She didn't know what to do, so she asked the guard to let her go to the leader and talk to him, but he said, "We don't have any doctors! Tell her how often people die!" She responded, "I know one doctor." The guard said, "He's not a doctor. He's a dentist." "All right. Let me go to him," my Mom said. And she took her there, but he said, "I'm not a doctor. I'm a dentist." But she told him, "You know what to do." He responded "But I don't have any equipment." My Mom said, "You have a knife. Just make it sterile."

"I don't have any pain killers. I don't have anything at all." And my Mom said to him, "Just cut it out." I sat on a chair, while two men held me down, and I screamed when he cut. They only had alcohol which was used in lamps (alcoholics used to drink it, so the Germans poisoned it with something), and they put this on my finger, which was bleeding, and then they put a strip from my dress around it. G-d was so good to me, and, after three or four weeks it healed. This is the finger; as you can see, the tip is missing.

I: Yes, I can see that quite clearly.

M: I was scared, so I went to work in pain because, otherwise, they would kill me. They would take us to the woods and make us dig ditches. They took out the sick people and shot them. It was just unbelievable.

We worked very hard. One day after work, my Mom was very, very sick with the typhus. I had typhus, too, but in a very light form because I had previously received the injection. I came back from work exhausted. All of a sudden, some Germans came in. "You! You! Come with us!" I didn't even reach my bunk bed. They put us on tracks where there were already some young men, and they gave us shovels, and we became very frightened when they took us to the woods, where we were forced to dig ditches. Behind us were Germans, the Einsatzgruppen, with guns pointed at us. That was how they killed people; they shot them in the back and let them fall into the ditches. I cried and prayed to G-d. I was too frightened to turn my head because I was afraid that they would kill me with those pointed guns.

We dug and dug. It was really late, and they started to holler, "Get back on the trucks!" We could hardly get back on the trucks—one person helped the other because we were so exhausted, and they took us back to the barracks. When we arrived, we crawled to the bunk beds, and, all of a sudden, we heard shooting, unbelievable shooting. We thought, What happened? Some of the girls said, "Oh, my G-d. You were digging those ditches for us; they are killing all the people in the barracks. The shooting goes on and on and on, and we will be the next ones who get killed." Everybody was talking; we didn't know what was going on, but we heard the shooting. As a matter of fact, they did take us out to a wooded place, a little space of land where the trees were not growing, at dusk. And there were so many people killed and bloody, dying wounded calling for help. And we had to watch this. They told us, "If you try to escape, that's what's going to happen to you."

My husband was one of those who survived this massacre—only three survived out of about four hundred. I mentioned before that we worked with Christians who were free people and who knew what was going on in the war. These Christians encouraged the men to escape from the camp because the Russians were coming very close to the camp. They said, "Why are you sitting and waiting for death. Get out!" So they tried to escape, but the soldiers killed them with machine guns. My husband was in the army before the war, and they taught him how to survive during a shooting: to throw himself on the ground and pretend that he is dead. And that was what he did. Then, other bodies fell on him. When night approached, he got to the woods, intending to go to his village. And he walked during the night and hid during the daytime. Out of four hundred, only three survived. I only knew this because he told me.

In the camp where we worked, we didn't wear any bands, but our clothes were marked with a red stripe in the back and the front of our clothes, so my husband was afraid to walk during the daytime. There were so many informers who would sell a Jewish soul for one kilogram of sugar. When he approached the village where he was born, he saw many Germans with torches, who were singing. "I must be crazy," he thought. He was hungry and utterly exhausted, but he decided to go back—as I said, at night he was walking, and during the daytime he was hiding.

In Poland at harvest time, the peasants had to cut the wheat with scythes. These women used to bring lunch for the men who were working in the fields, and in Europe they had a type of container that had three containers in one, and my husband saw such a container. A wife had gone to her husband to tell him that she had brought him some lunch, and my husband saw the container standing there. He got up, quickly grabbed the container, and ran because he was so hungry.

I: Let's keep to your experience, because it's what you witnessed firsthand. After this massacre that you witnessed, did you have to bury the bodies? Did you have to put them in the ditches?

M: Some people did. Those who were shot fell dead into the ditches. My husband started to walk back to the camp another five days, but nobody was in the camp anymore because they had sent us to Auschwitz in cattle cars. We traveled slowly—you could walk faster than the train was running—and were crowded like sardines, without water, without food. Sometimes Germans threw us food, but whoever was tallest grabbed the food. Whoever was tall could also breathe, because those cattle cars had cracks high up.

I: Were you with your mother and brothers then?

M: No. I didn't see my brothers anymore. They had separated us. I was just with my Mom, and all the time I tried to protect her with my body. She was a beautiful woman, and, whenever there was a selection, I pinched her cheeks so they would look red and she would seem healthy, and I tried to make her pretty. I said, "Bite your lips." And she made it through the selection. She was a young woman; after the war, she was only about forty years old. I tried to stand between her and the guards, and I pushed her.

So there was nobody in the camp when my husband came back. They had sent us to Auschwitz. So many people choked in the cattle cars; we didn't have any air, and we didn't have any place to sit. Sometimes we were happy just to be able to sit on a dead body. There were good people, too, but not too many . . . so few. I looked out through the little cracks, and I saw one peasant with a horse and a wagon full of cabbage; it was the fall harvest. And I heard him say in a loud voice, "Jesus Christ, help those people." And he started to throw leaves of cabbage, but nobody could catch them. He said, "Help them. Help them!" This made a great impression on me, and he came to my mind many times. I shall never forget it.

When we arrived in Auschwitz, we had to take out the dead bodies, and we had to get out. Right away, there was a selection. You have to remember that old people were not working; they had been singled out to die. And those who looked very bad, those were almost skeletons, were put aside. Those who looked better, who were more fit for work, they put on the other side. I was so happy that they put me with my Mom. They took us—there were young men and women—to a huge park, and they told us to undress completely; we were so humiliated. But there were some men standing over us with whips, so we undressed; we didn't know how to hide ourselves with our hands. Then they told us to sit and that we would get to shower. It was so arranged that you could see the entrance, but you couldn't see the exit from the shower. Therefore, we saw people going in, but we couldn't see them coming out. We were frightened and cried. Before we got to the showers, we were sitting naked on the damp ground because there was no floor. It took about six or seven hours before we got to the showers. Suddenly, I looked up and said to my Mom, "Tell me. What did I do to deserve this? What did we do?" She answered, "Nothing." I cried and prayed to G-d that water would come out of the shower heads. We were sure that they were going to gas us.

I: Had you heard about the gas in Auschwitz before you went there?

M: We heard about it. The Christians knew and told us. So I prayed to G-d, and, when water came out, I was so happy. It meant another few hours to live. The zest and drive for life was unbelievable. Everybody wanted to live; practically nobody committed suicide in camp. Before the war—before they went to the camps—some people did, but in the camp itself nobody committed suicide. Everybody wanted to live. They shaved our heads, put some DDT under our arms, and sprayed us all over.

Then they put numbers on our arms. It hurt terribly; it wasn't done as it's done now, by electricity. They just put a pen in ink and stuck us with it. They kicked and beat up those who complained or cried. Then they put us in barracks. When we got out and came to the barracks, they gave us slices of bread, but I could not eat the bread. I was starved, and the hunger was unimaginable. I started to vomit, but there was nothing inside to vomit. The odor from the burned flesh was terrible, and, when I looked up and I saw the flickering flames coming out from the chimney, I knew that those people had been gassed and burned. I couldn't eat, but my Mom cried "Eat! Eat!" But I didn't eat for maybe a day and half. Later, one got used to the odor, and I started to eat.

I: Is it a bad smell?

M: Yes. The smell's like barbecue. And, many times since, I can't stand a certain odor and don't want to eat because it smells like barbecue. It's a terrible odor, and when you look up and see the flames. . . . It's just unbelievable how cruel and inhuman one person can be to another, to have so much hate. We Jews didn't do anything wrong. We didn't even oppose their regime. We were obedient citizens, we paid our taxes, and our people served in the army. Some were scientists and very famous doctors who contributed so much to the civilization and culture of the world. Although we are a very small minority, the Jewish religion gave so much to others. But they singled out the Jews and the gypsies to die. How can people have so much hate?

I: Did you see gypsies in Auschwitz?

M: Yes, I did. I saw a camp with Jewish children and gypsies fenced in. I was a very courageous girl, and I remember that one morning I got up and looked out at a camp next to ours. We were fenced in with powerfully electrified wire; if you touched it, you were electrocuted. There were so many small children in the next camp who were crying after their brothers and their sisters. They called names. "Mom. Dad." I knew what was going to happen to them, but I didn't want to know. When I got back, however, I asked my Mom, "What are they going to do with those children?" Mom looked at me. "You want me to spell it out for you? Why?" And I cried and cried. Later, the next day, there weren't any children any more. So many flames came out of those chimneys. Because of my faith, I was thinking, "My G-d, maybe they would turn into angels." All that was left was a little hair, a handkerchief, or a shoe that the children dropped when they were taken. The camp was completely empty. They had burned two thousand children in one night, mostly gypsies and Jewish children. They had singled out the gypsies and the Jews to die.

It's true that they persecuted others—Jehovah's Witnesses, communists, socialists, homosexuals, lesbians—but not as much. For example, they gave them better food.

I: Did you meet any of the homosexuals in the camp yourself?

M: Yes. I guess they were homosexuals. In Auschwitz, I saw them, though I didn't meet them. Most of them were German citizens and were among the privileged, but they were put in the camp because they were homosexuals; they always walked with a little boy. They had better conditions. They got letters and packages with food from home. They selected a nice little boy, they dressed him nice, and they gave him a whip. If somebody didn't like someone else, he beat up this little boy, who was about ten years old.

In Auschwitz, they gave us some wooden shoes cut out from one piece, like the ones the peasants wore working in the fields in Holland. And sometimes when we walked it was muddy, damp, and so cold, and our shoe would stick in the mud. We didn't have strength to pull it out, so we left the shoe and walked with one shoe. Then, when we came back to the barrack, we started to exchange bread for a shoe. Some people had bread, but they walked barefoot.

They dressed people who worked in the chemical factory, IG Farbenindustrie AG, in striped uniforms. But most of us had hardly anything to wear. We didn't have underwear, just a dress. In Auschwitz, I have to admit, we didn't have any lice. They took us to the showers every week and put DDT on us. For hours, we had to sit and wait for the showers, but they did give us showers and another dress, which was clean and disinfected.

I: What actual food were you getting at this time? What did you have to eat?

M: Well, in Auschwitz, soup, a slice of bread, and coffee. It wasn't really coffee; I don't know for certain what it was.

I: This might sound like a stupid question, but what is it like to be very hungry, very starving? How do you feel?

M: How did I feel? I had a terrible pain in my stomach. Sometimes something sour came up in the beginning, but then, when I was starved to death and weighed fifty-five pounds, nothing came up. When we had just a little or no food, the fluid the stomach gave out in order to digest the food burned inside.

One day in Auschwitz, they put us in cattle cars and took us to Bergen-Belsen. We traveled five or six days. The indescribable road to Bergen-Belsen was worse than Hell. They didn't have gas chambers; they had a different method. They had crematoriums, but they could not consume all the bodies there were to burn, and skeletons were left outside—about fifteen thousand of them at the liberation.

We arrived at Bergen-Belsen, but most had died during the journey. I was again in the cattle cars, where there was no air. We were extremely exhausted—on our last leg—and the war had been going on about four years. Then, they opened up those cattle cars, and we had to get out, but we were too exhausted. When we finally made it to the ramp, they took us to our barracks. It was originally a military camp, but there hadn't been any soldiers for many years. The soldiers were on the front, and the peasants, Germans, and the villagers had completely dismantled the barracks. They took out the wooden floors, the shingles from the ceiling, the doors, and the windows. There weren't any bunk beds left besides the one which they built for the leader. And they put about three hundred women into a small barrack. We didn't even have room to stretch our legs. We sat cross-legged and supported each other back to back. They gave us food—a slice of bread and, again, thin soup—about once every other day. I remember them punishing us in Bergen-Belsen, but I don't know why; they didn't give us food or water for three days. We were sitting, exhausted, and, though we were not sleeping, we were unaware of what was going on. I remember that I sucked my finger until it bled.

Although I was so exhausted, I always wanted to know what was going on, so I crawled out of the barrack and said to my Mom, "I'm going to the kitchen." She said, "What kitchen? There is no food. Where are you going? You will die on the way." I said, "No. I won't," and I crawled and crawled until I got to the kitchen. There were containers with soup standing, but there was nobody to get the soup, and even ten of our starving people couldn't carry those containers. We did always carry a container for the soup with us, and we even slept with it; it held something like a quarter of a liter. I said, "Thank G-d. Soup. Soup." Nobody else was there, and standing before us were about twenty kettles of soup. I took off my container and dipped into the kettle. Because it had been standing maybe a day, it wasn't hot, and I sat on the ground and started to eat. I ate two containers and felt a little bit stronger.

I filled the third container with soup and said, "Now I'm going to take some to my Mom." When I came in, the whole barrack was as quiet as death, and it seemed that Death ruled. I held my Mom up, and I said, "Here's some soup." She said, "You're dreaming! You don't have anything in this container." I said, "This is soup! Why don't you eat? Here's a wooden spoon. Eat!" Then she started to eat, but the soup wouldn't go down, and half of it was running out of her mouth. I continued to feed her, and, when my container was completely empty, I went a second time to bring her more soup. I said, "Give me your container, too, and I'll bring two so we'll have some for later."

Then the people said, "Where did you get the food?" I said, "Get the soup. It's outside!" What happened was amazing. People were crawling for an hour to get to the soup, and some put their heads in the kettle, and—I'm not exaggerating—they drowned in the soup. Some did manage to get soup. This was in March. Then, once again, there was nothing for a few days.

It was almost the end of the war when we looked at the sky and saw the airplanes come. Bergen-Belsen was very close to big cities like Celle, Hanover, and Düsseldorf. It was such a joy to see the planes, because we always retained our hope. One day, we heard an alarm, but it didn't mean anything to us. The Germans had storage rooms with food in their kitchen, and they started to run to the bunkers. And they ran from the storage room to the bunker. I was outside with my aunt then looking at the planes, and I said to her, "Let's get in the storage room and get food! There is nobody! They ran like the rats! They're gone." And she said, "They'll kill us!" I said, "No, they won't!" and went to the magazine. There were steps. I just begun to walk up when I saw squares of margarine. Oh, my G-d, I hadn't seen margarine in so many years! It was a whole quarter of a pound. So I grabbed it, but I didn't know where to put it. I didn't have any underwear, but I had a dress, so I put it in the dress. Then I saw onions. You couldn't buy onions with gold or diamonds, because we valued its Vitamin C so much, and I took some onions. Then I saw sugar—but where to put it?—and some flour. I mixed the sugar with the flour. My aunt, who was older, said, "Come! Come! Don't take any more! Come! They will kill us! They will come back!" This happened in the woods where our barrack was, because they were hiding; the camp was a military camp. And then she said, "What are we going to do with the food? When we return to the barrack, they will kill us! Other people will take away the food!" I said, "Let's bury it." And we buried it. We dug and dug and put the margarine with the flour, with the sand. Every day I said, "Let's take out a little bit," and that's what we did. I never ever will forget that.

I: Did you ever see the camp commandant at Belsen?

M: Yes, I did. Hess was his name, and I saw him during the liberation. You cannot imagine it—we were eating raw flour. We didn't have any water; the water was outside and for some time had been frozen. There were swimming pools, but they were empty, except for rain water. It was full of mud and full of dead bodies. We were so thirsty; we walked a half day to the swimming pool. We couldn't really walk. We just shuffled our legs to get to the water.

But there was not enough water to scoop up in a container. Some people laid down and tried to drink, and that's the way how they drowned—in two inches of water!

In March, it's sometimes so cold that you cannot imagine, and the water outside was frozen. People were dying from a terrible, unbelievable epidemic of typhus. In the beginning, we didn't bury the corpses; we just put them out. But then, even six, or even eight, girls couldn't drag out the dead bodies.

Once in a while, once in two days, once in three days, we got food. Because this was at the end of the war, we didn't have any electricity. Instead of dividing the food into ten portions, our leader divided into fifteen, and she filled her stomach with the rest. She was pretty husky, or perhaps I should say, strong. She had swung back to observe what was going on. In the beginning, she forced us to carry out the corpses, but later she saw that we were dead bodies ourselves, that we could not do it; we were just skeletons, and she didn't bother us. Then, whoever died remained in the barrack with the living, and the odor was unbelievable. We didn't have the strength to get to the bathroom. And every day so many people died. During the daytime, we were talking. We were about eighteen or nineteen years old, and we were always talking about food and about how my Mom cooked this and how my Mom made this cake and I helped her. And we dreamt. My dream was that, one day, I'd be sitting at a table covered with a white tablecloth, and in the middle was a huge loaf of bread. There was nobody but me, and I'd take this bread and cut it in slices and eat and eat and eat! I was thinking about food all the time.

I: You know, people often talk about being hungry, don't they, and they say, "I'm starved." But when you are starving. . . .

M: You don't feel any more. You have no feelings.

I: Do you not feel a lot of pain?

170

M: No. You don't feel anything anymore. You just get dizzy and start to hallucinate. There's not enough blood getting to your brain. And I remember talking during the daytime with the other young girls. Whoever wasn't dead was talking. We supported each other back to back, because we didn't have enough space to stretch our legs. One day, I fell back, and I got angry at my friend Sarah. I said, "Sarah, when I want to get up, it takes me half an hour! Why didn't' you tell me that you wanted to move so I wouldn't fall?" She didn't answer. I said, "Don't you hear me?" She said nothing. I touched her, but she didn't answer. Then, I understood that she was dead. I didn't know what to do, and I continued to cry.

Next to me were beautiful twin sisters, who came either from Budapest or a little shtetl and who were very religious. They had reddish hair, naturally curly, and beautiful blue eyes. They were about sixteen or seventeen years old, and they were praying. During the daytime, sometimes I sat and talked to the girl next to me. She always spoke of the little town where she was born and about her parents. She was sitting, and I thought she was sleeping, so I touched her. Then, her sister said, "Don't you dare to touch my sister." I said, "What did I do? I just touched her." She said, "Don't touch her!" I asked why, and she said, "My sister is dead." She cried and prayed, and, about a half hour later, she died, too.

I: How did your mother bear up?

M: My mother was a bundle of bones and skin and weighed about forty-five pounds. I was so desperate! Around me, almost everybody was dead! It took me an hour of shaking and struggling to get up, and finally I touched my Mom. She seemed to be in a coma and did not respond, though she was not sleeping. Eventually, she gained consciousness and said, "What do you want now? What is it? Can't you sit and let us die in peace?" I said, "No. I don't want to die!" She said, "My dear child, it's easier to die than to live." I responded, "Mom, I am not going to die. Why should I die? I don't want to die!" She said, "Save your energy. Save your energy." Then, suddenly, I said, "Mom, I smell food." She said, "Where do you smell food? You're always talking about this and talking about that." I said, "Mom, I am going to bring you some food. Remember, I got you food twice." And she stated, "There is no food. There is nothing except death here." It took me a long time to get up, and I started to shuffle my legs inch by inch. My Mom cried, and she said, "You'll die on the way, wherever you're going. Don't go!" I got out to the hole where there once was a door, and I fell. It took me half an hour to get up. There were so many dead bodies—mere skeletons—scattered around. In Bergen-Belsen, when the British Army liberated us, there were about fifteen thousand skeletons outside. There were thousands of naked bodies. We either didn't have clothes or our clothes were falling apart. You didn't know what to do to cover yourself, and sometimes you were bleeding. So I walked. I got through the hole and stumbled over dead bodies, and I hurt my knee; I still have the scar. I walked, but I couldn't even hold my head straight because it was too heavy. I had to walk slowly, and every few inches I got sick. I had double pneumonia and tuberculosis. I was out of breath walking even slowly. Not too far, about forty yards from our barrack, was a kitchen for the German guards. And I smelled food. I looked up and saw a white flag on the kitchen roof. I talked to myself. "My Mom said I was crazy and was hallucinating, but I see the trees. I see the building. I see the windows from the kitchen. And I see some containers. Why would I see the white flag if it weren't on the roof? No," I said, "that is a white flag. But why is it there?"

I looked around and saw the Germans with their uniforms unbuttoned and not wearing any belts. They had white armbands. Next to them was a huge table with weapons. I said, "Nobody can tell me that this is not liberation. Nobody. Not even my Mom."

I didn't go for the food. I just went back to the barrack. It took me another hour and a half. When I arrived, with my last breath I said, "Girls! Girls! We are liberated!" They started to laugh at me and to spit on me. "You're crazy. You're imagining things. You never give up hope, do you?" And some—it took an hour for them to get up—raised their arms to beat me, but they didn't have the strength to do it.

We had a block leader in the barracks who heard me say "We are liberated!" She jumped down from her bunk bed and shouted, "You! What did you say? I heard you!" And my Mom started to plead, "Please, leave her alone. She's a sick girl. She's hallucinating. She doesn't know what she is saying." And I shouted to my Mom, "Yes I do! I do!" She said again, "No, she doesn't! Please leave her alone." She knew that I would die from one beating. And she said to me, "You see those skeletons, those dead bodies? You'll be one of them, if you're lying. What did you see?" I became so scared that I said, "I don't know anymore. I don't know." She said, "Mercy, if you lied." She jumped down and went out, and in two minutes she came back. "Oh, boy. She did not lie. We are liberated. We are liberated." And they started to laugh again. "You're crazy, too!" Everybody gave up hope. People were just sitting and waiting to die. Some were crawling out to die in the sun, to get a little bit of sun first.

This was the fifteenth of April. It didn't take long. Soon we heard over at the Red Cross shelter, "You are liberated. The British Army liberated you." This was proclaimed in five or six languages, because there were Jews from Hungary, from France, from Germany, from Poland, from Holland. The Jews said, "Oh, it must be a trick. It must be a trick." I told my Mom, "This is not a trick. Why don't you believe?" And finally she believed.

It didn't take long. About six British soldiers came in with their officer, and , with both hands, they covered their faces and closed their noses with their fingers because of the odor from dead bodies, which had been dead for weeks and were completely decayed. I never saw anybody crying as they did. The officer who was in charge said something like, "Jesus Christ! Why did you let this happen to people?" And he crossed himself. He said, "I've been in so many battlefields, I've buried my friends, but I never saw nor imagined seeing people like this." And he wept. He said, "Girls, what do you want?" Everybody answered, "Water. Water. We want water." Thirst is definitely worse than hunger. Our lips were completely split and dried out. I could even take out my teeth and hold them. I took one out and said, "I'm crazy, and I want to put it back in. I'm hallucinating." My Mom said, "What are you doing? Just leave it!"

And they went back, those soldiers, and brought containers with powdered milk and water. My Mom took the container away from me and said, "A little bit at a time!" I said, "Mom, I can eat! I can drink! But you won't let me! You want me to starve!" She said, "Please. Just a few drops at a time, a few drops at a time." And she took the milk away from me. She wouldn't let me drink too much.

Those soldiers went back and brought packages with their portions of food for the whole day. The packages contained Spam, biscuits, some kind of dried fruit, and chocolate. The soldiers started to distribute these, and people began to eat. You could also see those skeletons with the caved-in stomachs smoking cigarettes. You could see their stomachs start to fill in and bulge out. But, after an hour, everything came out both ways. Those people didn't survive. I would think fifty percent died from eating.

My Mom wouldn't let me eat, and I cried and hollered. She said, "Watch and see what happens to those people." I did, and soon I told her, "Mom, you're so smart."

We were in this barracks for another few days, then they put up field hospitals. They didn't have very many beds, so they put blankets on the grass on the ground. They carried us out in their arms because we couldn't walk, and they started to give us food to eat. There were doctors from Belgium, which was liberated before we were, who gave me only gelatin. And I said, "Gelatin! I don't want to eat any gelatin!" And my Mom said, "Eat! This is the right food for you. Eat." And then, little by little, they increased the food. They gave a tiny bit of milk, and so forth, and my strength came back. Then they burned Bergen-Belsen because of the lice. So many lice, and so many unburied bodies. Peasants were living around those camps not far away from our camp. The soldiers brought the whole village in and told them, "What did you do to those people? Didn't you know what happened?" And you know what they said? "Mein Gott. Wir haben gar nicht gewusst," which means, "Oh, my G-d. We didn't know anything about it." And the man, General Hughes, said, "You didn't know? You live so close, perhaps even less than a kilometer away! You walk by back and forth! You didn't know? What did you use those ashes for? To fertilize your farms? You didn't know?" And they helped to bury the corpses. They dug ditches with huge military tractors, and they put those skeletons in massive graves. Then they burned our camp.

There were people, mostly women from the Ukraine, who acted without pity. They killed other women and cut out their liver and ate it. I'm sorry. . . I don't want to talk about it.

It's in my nature to be curious, and I wanted to know see everything. I also like to help others, always help. I wanted to see the British troops. My Mom cried, "Stay! You can not even walk!" I said, "Mom, I have to see it. I have to." She warned me, "You'll die on the way." But, you know, hope can do so much to a person. I saw those Germans standing up in a line, and in charge of them was the commander, Hoess. And he said, "So many, many inmates, so many." He gave a report to Major Hughes—he was a major or general; I think a major that time. Hughes slapped him and said something, but I couldn't hear because I wasn't that close. The British troops were marching into the camp, and they wanted to see. And I saw one man who was half naked—a skeleton. Have you ever seen a person starve to death from hunger? Skin and bones. He shook and tottered when he walked. Then, he bent down and kissed the boots, the dusty boots, of the British soldier and told him, "If you came one day later, you would have found a completely dead camp." Then the man died. He couldn't get up any more. I didn't know the man, but I saw that they took him and laid him somewhere.

I: Maria, did you reach the rabbis who came in?

M: Yes. I did. This one rabbi, his name was Gringberg or Green-berg, I think. I remember that those who were left, the survivors, used to come. One day I visited some survivors whom they had put in a different camp. It was a tank school, a Panzer school. They burned Bergen-Belsen camp, you know, because there was a terrible epidemic; there were so many lice, and it was so dirty. In this Panzer school, this military camp, conditions were good, but still about eight people were housed in one room, but at least we had a room. We had beds and slept two in one bed. You got into the rooms through a hole in the wall. And there was a shower on one end of the bed and a toilet, and at the other end was a shower and toilet. At least we could wash ourselves with cold water. This was Hermann Goerring's headquarters in the Panzer school. So I spoke a little bit of English, I spoke French, and I knew German because I had had private tutors at home. And right away there were British women administrators from the military. There was a lady named Mrs. Steele who was looking for somebody who speaks English. They pointed to me. I couldn't speak English much, but I understood. Then we formed a Jewish Committee, and I was in charge of the information room and I worked there with Mrs. Steele, who was from the United Relief Organization, something like the United Nations now. I was paid a small amount in British pounds, and I worked for the Jewish community.

My Mom was so sick with tuberculosis all over her body—the lungs and the bones—that they sent her to Switzerland, where she was treated for seven years in a sanatorium. She was in Lucerne maybe a year and a half, and they thought that she was cured and sent her back to Bergen-Belsen, but she still had tuberculosis. Our countries didn't want to claim us or return our properties to us. (They clubbed eight hundred survivors in Poland to death. One friend of mine named Lieberbaum survived the war, but they killed him in Kielce. It was a very sorry world.) I remember, they took her to a hospital and made her ein Punktion; they stuck a heavy needle into her spine, and pus started to come out like a fountain. They didn't know what to do. They had some kidney-shaped containers, and one nurse called to the other, "Bring another one!" My Mom was in unbelievable pain, and they sent her back to Switzerland to a specialist for tuberculosis, the very famous Professor Rudier, who was about seventy-nine or eighty years old.

My Mom was a beautiful, very intelligent woman who spoke many languages. She was forty or forty-one years old then. Professor Rudier told her in French, "You have to live! I'll do everything for you." And he wrapped her like a mummy and put her in a Kausin bed. In the morning, they put many covers over her—she could only move with her arms—and placed her out on a terrace under the sun there in the mountains in Davost. She stayed a few years in this Kausinberg and recovered.

Professor Rudier's office was in Zürich. I accompanied my Mom when she went to visit him there. He never wanted any money. He had many people in the office, but he only wanted to see us. And my Mom said, "The people are sick; they are waiting for you." He was a very fine and courageous man.

Then my Mom lived in Switzerland, but she didn't have a Niederlassung, which you needed in Switzerland if you resided there but weren't a citizen. Without one, you could spend your money, but you weren't allowed to work. After seventeen years, you could get a Niederlassung; you wouldn't be a citizen, but you had the right to work, and you needed to report to the Police every so often. In the meantime, I worked for Mrs. Steele, whom I spoke about earlier.

The first time my Mom went to Switzerland, she was sitting at the window in bed. We put pillows around her because she didn't have the strength even to sit. She said, "I want to see my children coming." She was waiting. We didn't know what had happened to my two brothers, but she was waiting and waiting. And sometimes, we started to cry. "Oh, oh, that's him," but it wasn't. And one day my brother who was in Mauthausen came from Italy. After I had already been free a few days, the Germans gave my younger brother a gas shot in the heart, and that was how he died. A witness told us about this later; we survivors tried to inform each other.

I was working for Mrs. Steele for a few years and for the Jewish community and then decided to go back to Poland because I wanted our properties back and I wanted to go to school. Poland had a Communist regime then. When I arrived, I remember, I walked all the way from the railway station to the top of the big lodge because there weren't any cars. Poland was not a great developed country like England or France. It was in the evening, and, when the night approached, I didn't have anywhere to go. I sat in the street all night. In the morning, I thought that there must be a Jewish community somewhere near. When I asked people, they said, "You're Jewish. What are you doing here? Didn't Hitler kill all of you?" Then someone walked by and said to me, "I'll take you." It was a Jewish community. They told me to go to Magistracze 24, where some survivors lived. My dear husband was one of them. He had graduated in law before the war and then went for another degree. There were perhaps twenty or thirty people living in two rooms. My husband told me he got this apartment with his sister, but everyone came because they didn't have any relatives nor anywhere to stay; they were alone. When I arrived there, they told me that I could stay. So I went to the high school and then to college. In the meantime, we married, and we had two wonderful daughters. My brother who survived Mauthausen traveled to the

United States and lived here in St. Louis. He had been writing letters to me and sending packages—life wasn't very good in the Communist countries. One day, I told my husband I just had to leave. We applied to go to Israel, but they rejected because we were educated people. So I decided to visit my brother. My husband told me I was crazy. "They won't give you a passport!" They had rejected us so many times us when we wanted to go to Israel. But I needed to leave, and I applied for a passport, and the O.B, the military police came and took me. My husband said, "I told you not to apply." So they took me and started to ask me questions. They told me., "You're a spy." I denied it and said, "If you had a brother, the only brother who had survived, wouldn't you write letters to him? Wouldn't you apply to see your brother?" They insisted I was a spy, interrogated me for two hours, and had me in tears. When I came home, my children had missed me, and my husband said, "I told you not to do it, but you don't want to listen! Now what's going to happen to us?" After a few weeks, they took me and accused me again of being a spy. I said, "You can beat me. You can torture me. I was not and am not a spy. I will never sign any statement that I'm a spy because I'm not." Then I said, "Are you really a Communist? You know, I read Marx's books. Communists shouldn't treat people as you're treating me! Why are you treating me like this? I'm not a spy." Then they told me to go into another room. Then one of them came and told me I could leave, and I walked home. After another month, they took me again. A woman at a desk spoke accusingly. "We know you're a spy! You're getting packages from America and from Switzerland! You have connections. We know that you are a spy." (My Mom had sent the packages from Switzerland.) I said, "I have connections only with my Mom and with my brother. They send me food. What's bad about that!" And then she looked at me and said, "If we will give you a passport, are you going to spy?" "For whom?" I said. "I just want to go to see my brother." "You'll get a passport," she said. "We'll give you two papers: one paper for you and one for your husband." This paper stated that I would never ever have claim to my family if I returned because I applied for a visa. My husband's paper stated that he would never claim me; I would be dead to him and to the children. When I gave him the paper, he said, "Do you think I'd sign a paper like this? I won't let you go." I carried on for maybe a week before he'd sign it. They accepted it and gave me the passport. I traveled to the United States, actually to Canada, on the ship Batory. From Canada, I took a plane to the United States and asked for asylum, which was granted. I had been in touch with Senator Symington from Missouri. There was a law that I couldn't bring my family here. (I'm sorry to say that America didn't do much for Jews, either. They hadn't let in twenty thousand children; they had turned back a ship called the St. Louis which held German Jews, but that's another story.) I was crying day and night. I bathed and got ready to go to work, but Mans, my brother, would not let me go to work. But I said, "I have to work." I have to be occupied. Otherwise, without my family, I will go crazy." So I got a job and worked for an exquisite store dealing exclusively in ladies clothing. When they closed this store, I went to work for the May Company at Famous-Barr. I became a manager of the alterations department, designed beautiful clothes for the mighty, and worked there twenty-seven years. When they changed the law after nine months, I immediately sent for my family, and they came over.

My husband attended Washington University for his diploma, though not as a lawyer, because one had to have mastered the English language. Instead, he graduated in business administration and passed the test as a certified accountant. When he became a citizen, he worked for the American army and was in charge of the whole accounting. I worked eighteen hours a day so that my husband could complete his certification and because we didn't have much money. When they let us leave Poland, they gave five dollars in exchange. Five dollars! My husband walked to Washington University to save a quarter in bus fares. I walked to save fifty cents to Famous-Barr in Clayton.

When my mother found out that they had let me my family come to the U.S., she sacrificed and came here from Switzerland. She recovered after ten years and had a very good life later as well as wonderful and influential friends, some among the intelligentia—Mr. Mercing, for example, who was in charge of the Masons in Switzerland. But she sacrificed everything and came to be with me and my brother.

I: You spoke about your mother and her T.B. Have you had any long-term illness?

M: Yes. I did. When they gave me the pass to leave Poland and come to this country, you have to undergo a medical examination, and I went to Warsaw for mine. There was only a consulate, not an embassy, because the Communist countries didn't have connections with the United States. So they examined me and took some x-rays. Then they told me to go back home and said they would let me know. After four weeks, word came that I would not be allowed to go to United States, and I broke down in tears. I had tuberculosis on both of my lungs. They said they were going to send my Roentgens to Paris, where there was an American embassy. In the meantime, my sister-in-law—my husband's sister—who was a doctor said, "Don't cry. I'll take you to my friends who specialize in lung disease. You are not in pain, and you have healthy children. Why are you crying so much?" And she took me to a doctor friend, and when he examined the Roentgen he took, he said, "How can you live? How can you breathe? Your lungs are completely deteriorated." I said, "I can breathe all right." I returned home, and I cried that night. In the morning, my husband said, "I'll take you to Dr. Cherouchevky, a friend of ours. He was a doctor in the military after escaping from Russia and has a big practice." Dr. Cherouchevky did come, and he said to me, "Don't cry. If you were so sick, you wouldn't be able to go to the theater or to the symphony or to run around and play with the children. You would be spitting up blood. You cannot be that sick. Come to my office," he said. As would have been the case in Poland, where doctors seldom had a private practice, he worked in a hospital. They took an x-ray. He looked at it and explained, "You had tuberculosis, but it's completely healed. Only the scars remain." In the meantime, I waited for the results, from the embassy in Paris. They confirmed our doctor's diagnosis; I was healed and healthy. That's how I came here.

I: Do you have any ill effects today, though, Maria? Do you have any health problem today which trace to the camp?

M: Yes. Yes. I have some terrible problems. They were treating me for allergies and sinuses for fifty years, but nothing helped. I had arrhythmia, and my heart weakened. I wanted to exercise but didn't want to take Seldine, the medication which was prescribed, but I was getting so weak that I couldn't walk. About ten years ago, I told my husband, "I'm not going to take the medication any more." I went to our internist, who examined me and told me I had a bad heart. This Seldine had terrible side effects. I stopped taking it, and, about a half year later, I called the doctor and told him. He said, "You have heart troubles and should take the medication. The medication's fine." I had read a Time magazine article warning that Seldine had terrible side effects, that sixty people on it had died, and that many people have side effects, like arrhythmia. I went to the doctor, who monitored my heart for quite a while. When I stopped taking it, the doctor was surprised, but my heart improved.

My husband had heart problems, too, so we went to the Mayo Clinic. Since I was there with him, I told the doctors about a health problem of my own for which no medication helped. I was sent to Professor Desoto, who was training doctors for the Mayo Clinic. And he made an allergy test and said that I had no allergy problem. He said, "You know; I've treated quite a few survivors who came from Canada and from other cities. They had the same symptoms as you, and I decided to research it with a few doctors. I'll engage a few doctors, and we'll have the research. We came to the conclusion that your glands did not develop. You were young in the Nazi camps. You didn't have any vitamins or minerals, and you didn't get enough food. I've developed a medication, but I don't give you any guarantee that it will help. It's called Aesius, and I'll it give you because you can't buy it anywhere." I was very grateful, and I took the medication. When I told him it wasn't helping me, he said, "I'm sorry. I cannot put new glands in you." That's what I have. I choke all the time. Right now, I have a frog in my throat because the mucous is hard and sits in my throat.

I: Both you and your husband are survivors, Maria. Do you think that has affected your children?

M: Yes. Definitely. My children are very sensitive and good-hearted. They would give away everything if someone needed it. They are both artists and are very educated. One daughter graduated in psychology; then, she went back to school and graduated from the Washington University art school. The other daughter won a scholarship to Cooper Union, one of the best schools in the world. She was the only graduate from the art school who was awarded a monetary prize. The dean exchanged pictures with her, and he took us out when she graduated. Though she could have made a fortune in graphic art, she only wanted to study fine art, though she didn't want to teach art.

I: But would you say they were they affected in any way by the Holocaust? Were they disturbed by it, or do you think being Holocaust survivors made a difference in your parenting?

M: No. We were very protective, and it hurt them that we had suffered, and they never wanted to hear about our suffering. My younger daughter, the psychologist, said, "Talk, Mom! Get out of your system. That is your medicine, your best medicine." And it did help me.

My husband used to speak about the Holocaust. He is a brilliant man, but always depressed. He reads day and night. Between the books we have upstairs and downstairs, we own a whole library.

I: Had you not spoken about the Holocaust until your daughter urged you to?

M: No. I had always tried to speak to others, but they didn't want to listen. They would say, "Why do you talk about what was? You are in the United States now." They didn't want to listen. I won't mention names, but I remember one very learned woman presented a lecture quite a few years ago. She said, "Oh, the survivors didn't want to talk about it." I stood up and disagreed. I said, "I beg your pardon. We did not want to talk about it? You people didn't want to listen to us. You did not want to listen." And then a man stood up and said, "I was in the army and I fought. I liberated Buchenwald. But, when I try to tell people, they don't want to listen to me. This lady is right. They want to talk, but you people don't want to listen." A few didn't want to, but ninety percent did want to talk.

I: I know you give a lot of talks at the Holocaust Museum and Learning Center. Why do you do that?

M: The world has to know. The world has to know. Nobody stood up for us. People were indifferent, and that indifference is the largest killer. It isn't only those who kill, but those who are indifferent. You have to stand up for other people's rights. Human beings are created the same way. We have different faiths. Some have different skin color skin. But essentially we are the same, and the same red blood flows in everyone's veins. You don't have to associate with someone you don't like, but you have to respect everybody. If you respect, you'll be respected. I don't know why some people have so much hate in them. They hate themselves, so they hate others, too. They hate themselves.

I: Finally, Maria. What are your feelings about Germany today? Have you forgiven?

M: I did not forgive, and I have not forgotten. However, there is another generation now, and those young people are not at fault. Perhaps ninety percent of Germans are at fault and acted willingly, voluntarily. They were anti-Semitic and seemed to enjoy it. Those were a learned people who loved music and books and loved their pets. I shall never understand how they did what they did, how inhuman one person can be to another. I'll tell you this much; I don't hate anybody. I really don't. But I cannot forget and I cannot forgive. There is no excuse for killing with premeditation. This was figured out. At the Wannsee Konferenz, they agreed to the Final Solution. Then they had drinks and had lunch. So, can you forgive or forget? What kind of people were those? Yet, they say they had orders. They had orders to kill somebody. Order me to kill somebody, and I'll say, "No." How can I kill a person? I cannot even hit a person. I cannot step on a bug, so help me G-d.

I: Maria, thank you very much indeed for telling me about your experiences and for sparing so much time for the Imperial War Museum.

M: You know. Everybody has different experiences, and you should not compare one survivor to another. Some Jews, for example, were in labor camps in Warsaw, but they were free.

I: Do you think you can ever really describe what happened, and other people really understand?

M: There aren't adequate words in the dictionary. You have to form new words, special words, and not misuse them. People speak loosely of a Holocaust in Yugoslavia. But, in Yugoslavia, those people are free. They farm their land. They live in their homes. They carried weapons. They can defend themselves. They're not fenced in. They live, and they fight a war against each other! The Jews did not start a fight with anybody. They were obedient citizens who paid their taxes and served in the military. In Poland, a Jew could not work in or for the government. A Jew couldn't be a policeman or a firefighter. A lot of Jewish people were starving. Although they worked as shoemakers, tailors, carpenters, and in all kinds of professions, they were dying of hunger and starvation. No. There aren't any words. There will never be.

Sometimes still, as I sew or design or write, I think about it all in disbelief. I think to myself, "Are you stupid? Can you believe it happened?" You can hardly believe yourself. You can hardly believe your own eyes.

Maria Szapszewicz

Appendix

Maria Szapszewicz

Barely Living in the
Dystopia of the Holocaust

For obvious and grisly historical reasons, the name of the Polish town Oswiecim has to the ears of most people bęen supplanted by the German name Auschwitz. The ghettoes of Warsaw and Lodz, however, have retained their Polish names. Maria was born in the city of Lodz to Sara and Majlech Wajchendler and had two brothers. Their family cherished education and was both religious and progressive. The father and one son were to perish in the Holocaust, but Maria and her mother ultimately, by luck or will power or quizzical Providence, survived the atrocious juggernaut of the Nazi ideological machine.

Maria lived in both the Lodz and Szydlowiec ghettoes and was forced to work in an ammunition factory in Starachowice. For the five-year duration of the war, she and her mother were incarcerated and made to work at Auschwitz and Bergen-Belsen concentration camps and were liberated, barely alive, from Bergen-Belsen on April 15, 1945, weighing fifty-five and forty-six pounds respectively. Her mother was to undergo seven years of treatment in a sanatorium in Switzerland for tuberculosis. Soon after Maria regained her health, she helped organize the Jewish community, assisted organizations formed to help survivors establish new lives, and worked in a displaced persons camp.

Three years later, she returned to Poland to claim lost family property and to investigate the status of her family. The then-Communist Polish government had confiscated family lands and refused to allow Maria the right of egress once she had entered the country. She made the best of a poor situation by returning to her schooling and finishing high school and college. She married Jacob Szapszewicz and had two daughters, Rose and Joanne, who studied psychology and art. She also began to write articles for Polish magazines. Finally, in 1959, after repeated rejections of her requests to leave Poland, based largely on the diagnosis that she had active TB, she was permitted to emigrate to the U.S., where she continued to do volunteer work for the Jewish community, worked professionally as a seamstress in one major store, and eventually had a highly successful twenty-seven-year career as fashion advisor and manager of the alterations department in the Famous-Barr department store which acclaimed businessman, philanthropist, and art collector Morton May had built. More recently, she has been one of the mainstays of the group of docents and lecturers at the Holocaust Museum and Learning Center in St. Louis, where she speaks almost daily to a wide variety of groups of all ages—from the most innocent of elementary school children to the most experienced of state troopers.

In settings in which she shares her poetry, those who hear her will understand that Maria wants "to know/Why our chosen people had to die,/And my heart will always cry/Until the day when I, too, shall die" ("For Those Innocent People I Loved"). She indeed often begins her presentations, "You have the privilege of hearing the testimony of a Holocaust survivor," thereby calling attention to the simple fact that firsthand witnesses of the Holocaust are passing away. She reminds us that "We survivors of the Holocaust are dying one by one./Each day there are fewer of us left" ("The Last Remnants"). "Nazi-hunter" Simon Wiesenthal has noted that he has outlived most of the perpetrators he has hunted for five decades and is now attempting in his retirement to catalogue a vast store of information and research so it can be utilized for decades to come. It is indeed a particular and dear privilege to hear another rare entity, Maria as Holocaust poet, give voice to her reflections, memories, and feelings of those most bitter times.

Maria's verses are nourished by a fertile mix of personal remembrance, historical research, and poetic response. In "The shtetl," she depicts the town where she visited her grandmother many years ago and in which her mother was born. In "The Hiding Place," the speaker's voice is that of her husband Jacob, who was indeed encyclopedic in his retention of his immense reading; Maria's poem is a tribute to Jacob, who long ago wanted to protect his book from the ravages of an approaching storm and hid it under a rock. Jacob's sister recently found the book. It survived, but in an utterly disintegrated condition, and she was unable to decipher the book's contents. Another of the many poems dedicated to her husband, "For the Unknown Partisan," in part eulogizes the work of her husband, who was one of those partisans.

When she posits what are arguably rhetorical questions, ones for which some readers may yet attempt to venture answers, the integrity of her utterance and the seriousness of the issues point the hearer to alternate responses, the most valuable being that of listening. When one is privileged to hear a witness, one must listen; there is no other adequate basic response. Once the poem is heard, then one may weigh the variety of responses that may suggest themselves. She closes "The Crimes of the World," for example, with the words: "On the other side of the fence lies a beautiful world/Where people are free./Why? We Jews/couldn't fit this world./We were singled out to die./Why does the world commit such a crime?" It is, of course, possible to try to fathom why some would "commit such a crime," but such a literal answer is ill-suited to a prophetic proclamation. In Maria's voice one can easily hear the prophet. Hers is often the eloquent cello voice in Ernest Bloch's musical poem *Shelomo*. It is helpful to remember that the root etymology of the word prophet deals with speaking on behalf of another, and usually, in biblical literature, on behalf of the Deity. Maria's utterances are rendered on behalf of a nigh-annihilated people, on behalf of humanity, on behalf of the future, and veritably indeed, for many, on behalf of G-d. In "Music and Songs," Maria examines something left behind, the songs of the survivors. "With those songs, they went to death./But we will remember them;/They are in our hearts forever./As long as we will live,/They will live too." One should look in Maria's poetry, and in any truly significant poetry, for a richness of voice and purpose. Look for beauty, look for truth, look for experience, look for feeling, look for direction, and look for the possibility and the likelihood of prophecy.

Admittedly, Maria retains many memories which have not yet found a voice. There are horrors about which she has not yet found the words or the desire to speak. There are the still-silent scars left on her body by the riding crop with which Dr. Mengele struck her. There are the recollections of and affections for so many of her dear friends who did not reach liberation alive, who succumbed to TB, to typhus, to starvation, or to the weapons of their murderers. Yet Maria nonetheless manages to tell us so much. She remains, in spite of the bracing and sobering content of much of her poetry, a complex poetic voice of compassion, of accusation, of judgment, of love, and of rebuilding, and there will be few hearers who cannot sense the presence and the power of each of these elements. It is our privilege to hear, to remember, and to respond to her words. May we listen and learn so that people may no longer be oppressed, treated as nonentities, or annihilated in the yet-unwritten pages of human history. May humanity learn from a sensitive study of the biblical book of Genesis to write its future without following the Divine Creator's life-giving acts with brother murdering brother. May each of us be co-writers of that history.

Robert J. Hutcheson, Ph.D.

Editor's Afterword

I first met the author in the summer of 1999, when she spoke in St. Louis as a member of a Holocaust panel at a Yad Vashem workshop for teachers. Maria's intensity and burning faith, not to mention her honesty, her expressiveness, and the warmth of her fairness, particularly impressed me. After the session, we spoke a bit, and she gave me two of her poems. That was when I became aware of her passion for poetry. I still find it remarkable that, an hour or so earlier, during her panel talk, I was feeling poetic buzzing galore and felt the need to sit down and write a poem as a response of gratitude to her. I sent her that poem, and we have remained personal and poetic friends since that day.

The following spring, Maria spoke at my high school to students whom the State labels "gifted." These are students who are familiar with Elie Wiesel, with Chaim Potok, with burning ethical issues, and with the need to address inequities of all types. As she shares, Maria often speaks with her eyes closed and with an expressive voice, remembering vividly for the umpteenth time the love of her mother, the death of her brother, the deprivation, the hunger and the anguishing torture of those days of her youth. The students sat moved and enrapt during the hour of her talk. Some of them told their parents about the experience, and some of those parents wept.

It is true that Maria has some physical discomfort in her speaking. The camp years, when she was fifteen to twenty years old, and the nutritional deprivations of those years, caused thwarted development in her glands, and she can scarcely salivate. Though her voice is not raspy or feeble, her throat remains dry, and she tends to cough; it remains a living vestige of the malice and cruelty of which she is an eloquent witness.

A strange irony speaks to us from her memories of Auschwitz. Maria's persecutors seemed forever to be drawing blood from her and the other prisoners. Was the blood of the Jews going to the front lines to help wounded, pure Aryan-blooded German soldiers heal and survive. Maria has traveled the road toward healing, and she has done so much more than simply survive. The charismatic power of her words and experience have not been stilled by time nor by her emotional and physical scars. Her voice resonates, too, with love and healing. May her words continue to bring healing to all of her hearers, to each of us, to all of us.

Robert J. Hutcheson, Ph.D.

Maria Szapszewicz